Taxi Tales

Lou Solitske

ISBN:1540699684
ISBN-13 9781540699688

THIS BOOK IS DEDICATED FIRST AND FOREMOST TO MY LONGSUFFERING WIFE AND PARTNER IN LIFE JACKIE.

AS WELL AS, ALL THOSE STRANGE AND WONDERFUL PEOPLE WHO RIDE AROUND IN CABS IN THE WEE HOURS OF THE NIGHT.

AND LASTLY TO THE MEMORY OF LITTLE RICKY WHO I AM SURE IS RAISING HELL IN POODLE HEAVEN.

ACKNOWLEDGMENTS

Many Thanks To:

Fred and Kenny Pleines for their patience, understanding, support, trust, friendship, and for giving me a home at Yellow Cab for all these years. Jerry Perry and Jack Barnes for their technical support. Jay Spooner for the cover photo John Vasconcellos for suggesting the title. Ray Taliaferro of KGO Radio for giving me the opportunity to inflict my poetry on the entire west coast and last but not least, to Heidi Schiavone and LaurieAnne Blanchard who have toiled with me, encouraged me, fought with me, educated me, inspired me more than they will ever know and have kept this book from being one incredibly long run-on sentence.

TAXI TALE

All night long I roam these streets
Picking up drunks, sweethearts and freaks
Night after night I am in my car
Rushing to the hospital
Or sitting and waiting in front of some bar
Night after night I am in my car
Hauling around strangers can really get bizarre
Sometimes I'm bored, sometimes I'm scared
Sometimes I'm listening to a heart being bared
But all night long I roam these streets
Looking for those drunks, sweethearts and freaks.

Introduction

I have been a night driver for Sacramento Yellow Cab since 1987. Right off the bat I found myself in bizarre, humorous, sad, thought-provoking, and scary situations. Friends and passengers enjoyed hearing about my adventures and often asked me if I had any new stories. After a while it occurred to me that if people enjoyed hearing about these encounters perhaps they would like reading them as well. I started writing them down and eventually it became obvious to me that there were enough tales to make a book.

Chapter 1.

I have come to the conclusion that the consumption of alcohol does not necessarily promote deep thinking. Once again, this concept was about to be reinforced in spades by the fellow riding next to me in my cab. We were on our way to pick up his girlfriend after which we would go to Lake Tahoe. "This is just to show you I'm for real," he said, handing me a hundred-dollar bill. He had quite a sense of humor, and thus far I had been enjoying the ride.

He appeared to be in his mid-sixties, a small firecracker of a man, who undoubtedly left a wake of mayhem and destruction behind him wherever he went. He was consuming great quantities of vodka straight from the bottle as we drove through that early July evening.

It's a little-known fact that drinking in a cab is legal, as long as I'm not the one doing the drinking. Section 23229.0 of the California Vehicle Code exempts tour buses, limousines and taxicabs from the open container provisions prohibiting people from drinking in cars. I don't mind hauling around drunk people; I would much rather have them in the cab with me than on the road with me.

He spotted my cellular phone and asked to call his lady friend. I punched in the number he told me, hit the send button, and handed him the phone.

"Myrna, this is Hank. I'm on my way over. My buddy Lou is going to take us up to Tahoe."

I couldn't hear her exact reply, but she was clearly asking him to leave her alone.

"Don't give me that crap," he was shouting. "We're almost there. We're gonna break down the door and take you with us if we have to!" Well, this was certainly becoming an interesting cab ride.

Although there was no way I would be party to a kidnapping, I did decide to let this drama play out at least a little further. Before long we arrived at an apartment complex catering to retired folks. At the main entrance, we encountered the largest human being I have *ever* seen in the flesh. The man was at least 7 feet tall and must have weighed over 400 pounds. I kid you not. He was huge. He seemed to fill the entire doorway. He was talking into a two-way radio as we arrived. Undeterred, Hank got out of the cab and stomped up to the door. The man came out and said in a booming voice, emphasizing each word with the force of a gale, "The lady wants you to leave her alone! If you do not leave immediately, I will call the police!

If you ever come back, I will call the police!"

Hank scurried back to the relative safety of the cab, where he immediately took another slug of vodka, and had an alcohol-inspired thought.

"Hey, I'm not going to let that big nigger shove me around. I'm gonna take him on. You're gonna back me up, right?"

"I'll take you to the hospital when he's through with you if you're still alive," I replied. "I figure it's an even-money bet unless you call him a nigger. You do that and we will need the medical examiner to determine the exact cause of death."

"Hey, I used to be a Marine!" he shouted with great conviction.

"This guy could be an entire Marine battalion," I shouted back, pointing in the direction of the massive black hulk looming in the doorway. His malevolent, angry eyes never left us.

"Do you really want to antagonize HIM?" I asked somewhat heatedly.

Hank sulked and drank all the way home. Although I didn't get to take him to Tahoe, I did have the satisfaction of watching him stagger to his front door on his own two unbroken legs.

Chapter 2

As I pulled into the parking area for the emergency room at Sutter General Hospital, I saw a woman looking keenly in my direction. She started walking towards the cab. I quickly sized her up. She was in her seventies, trim and spry. There was brightness in her eyes that belied her years. I switched the radio to classical music. I find that appropriate music can contribute to the enjoyment of a cab ride -- I strive to provide a pleasant environment. I like to think that I give good cab.

As it turned out, my choice of music was very appropriate. The woman hurried to the cab and jumped into the front seat. She lived in West Sacramento. Once she settled in, I made the half-witted observation that she sure knew how to have fun on a Thursday night. She laughed and said that she sure did since she had spent the last four hours at the emergency room.

I never question the circumstances

when picking up at a hospital or a jail. I figure that if they want to talk about it, they will. Some do; this lady didn't. I offered her a piece of gum. When she declined, I said, "Mom told you not to take candy from strangers, huh?" Again, she laughed. She seemed to enjoy my feeble attempts at humor. This is a routine I have developed to help make people feel more comfortable in my presence. I stand about 6'2" and weigh 275 lbs. I wear black boots, black pants, a black shirt, a black leather vest, black fingerless gloves, and a black Fedora. All in all, it's not a pretty sight. My attire and demeanor are designed to project the image that I would be more trouble than I'm worth. Unfortunately, I go places where looking like "Guido the Detroit Hit Man" helps keep me alive a little longer. In an attempt to overcome the menacing image I portray I offer my passengers gum and try to make them laugh. People like to laugh, and they like people who make them laugh.

The music helps as well. We were listening to an excerpt from Bizet's Carmen. My passenger happened to be

French and sang along with the music in a clear, strong voice. I thoroughly enjoyed the performance. I asked her if she knew the Marseillaise (the French National Anthem).

"But, of course!" was her reply.

I turned off the radio and she launched into one of the most incredible renditions of the Marseillaise that I have ever heard. It gave me goose bumps and brought tears to my eyes. When she finished and looked at me, she was touched that she had so moved me. She asked why I had reacted that way and I told her that the song had great historical significance to me.

When the allied armies were about to liberate Paris, Eisenhower assigned the task to the Free French Corps commanded by Charles De Gaulle. The Germans retreated and fortunately did not put up much of a fight. When DeGaulle and his troops entered the city, the entire population poured into the streets to greet them. I have seen newsreel footage showing DeGaulle leading what must have been all of Paris plus his liberating forces in singing that stirring anthem. Just as they concluded a sniper opened fire barely missing DeGaulle. But missed he did.

Ever since I saw that film, the Marseillaise has occupied a very special place in my heart. I relayed the story to my French passenger and she seemed surprised. She said she had been there that day and it was one of the most moving days of her life. She was amazed that I, who was obviously not even alive at the time, should be so intimately aware of what happened.

I explained that history was one of my passions, and told her it was a real thrill for me to talk with someone who participated in such an historic event. I asked if she was in the Marquis (the French Resistance) and she answered affirmatively. Now I was really excited. She unfortunately did not want to talk about her wartime experiences, and although I was disappointed, I respected the woman's wishes, realizing that for some people remembering the war was simply too painful.

It was, however, very frustrating for me to be so close to a first-hand historical source such as this, yet be denied her recollections. I wondered what roll this diminutive figure next to me, wearing her beret, had played in the history that was made so long ago, so very far away.

Chapter 3

She couldn't have weighed more than 80 pounds. She came to the front door of the cab, which I opened from the inside. As she got in, she was illuminated by the dome light. Her flesh hung on her bones her skin was translucent. There were bruises on her arms from the many needles she had recently endured. She only had a few patches of her hair left. When she closed the door, the dome light mercifully went off. She had been sitting on her neatly made twin bed, the door to her single room in the dingy West Sacramento bungalow wide open. She lived alone. She appeared to be in her mid to late forties, although I'm sure that her recent ordeal had aged her substantially.

She asked me to take her to Kaiser South. This would be a long ride. Normally, I would be worried about getting paid in this neighborhood, but I had already decided that in this case money was not a matter of concern, and that this woman, obviously dying of cancer, would get to the hospital regardless of her ability to pay.

I had just returned home from visiting my parents in Los Angeles, where my father had undergone exploratory surgery and, like my passenger, was found to be riddled with cancer. He had been given two months to live, at best. More than anything, my father wanted to go home. I will never forget the day he was released from the hospital. Hunched over in that wheelchair, his wrinkled bald head gleaming in the overhead light, he was rolled down the corridor to the car that would take him home for the last time.

My mother had given him a simple promise: She would keep him odorless, spotless, and pain-free. With help from the wonderful people at the hospice outpatient program, she did just that. One quiet, peaceful afternoon, my father slipped away in his sleep, in the home he loved, with the woman who had been his partner in life, for more than 55 years at his side. I have never witnessed a greater expression of love than as I watched that 74 year-old woman care for that 79 year-old man.

As we sped through the night, heading towards Kaiser South, classical seemed the most appropriate choice of music. I switched on the radio and asked my passenger if she minded.

"What do I care what kind of music you want to listen to. I'm dying," she blurted out. With that she began to cry.

"Do you need a hand to hold?" I asked tentatively.

"Desperately," she sobbed.

I removed the glove and offered my right hand to her. She reached out and clutched it. Then she began to cry even harder. Now I was crying as well; the tears streamed down my cheeks, a single cello playing mournfully on the radio suitably accompanied the sorrow that filled my cab.

"I'm so frightened," she said. Then she turned and looked at me.

"Is this all there is?" she asked, as though she expected me to have the answer. Oddly enough, I did. At least it was 'an' answer.

"I believe...I fundamentally believe...that there is a lot more going on here than what meets the eye. I believe that normally we exist in the spiritual realm, simply some form of energy, emotions, intellect and who knows what else. But without form or substance, maybe outside of dimensions or time as we know them. Every once in a while, our spiritual entities get to put on the body of a human being and come down to earth to have a sensual vacation; one where we can experience the delights to be found in the physical world. The purpose of life, therefore, is not to inflict senseless pain and suffering on ourselves and everyone around us. The purpose of life is to experience and be experienced; to enjoy and be enjoyed; to learn and to teach. When our vacation is over, we leave our withered bodies behind and return to the spiritual realm with our memory banks filled with our earthly adventures. Then we resume our normal spiritual existence, broadened by those experiences from the physical realm."

My passenger had stopped crying. She was looking at me as though she had received some sort of divine revelation.

"Do you really think that's how it's going to be?" she asked hopefully.

"I intuitively believe what I just told you to be true," I said with conviction.

"If I'm wrong, and there is nothing after this life, then you're not going to know the difference anyway. But if I'm right, then you are about to embark on a most remarkable adventure. Be curious."

I gently squeezed her hand.

"It certainly is a mystery," she said with a faint smile and a faraway gleam in her eyes as she slowly shook her head. She almost glowed. I will never forget the look on that face as it uttered those words. Shortly thereafter we arrived at Kaiser South. She wanted to know how much she owed me.

"Nothing," I replied.

"Wrong," she said, "I owe you more than you'll ever know." She leaned over and kissed my cheek, then headed for the hospital entrance.

Yes, it certainly is a mystery, I thought to myself. I never saw her again.

Chapter 4

I was cruising Old Sacramento, trolling for fares. Three people flagged me down: Two women and a man. They were older folks, and took a while to get into the cab. They were all dressed up and one of the women climbed into the front seat. She was wearing furs and diamonds. They were headed to Chargin's, a small neighborhood bar, at 49th and J.

They had all been drinking and as we took off, my front seat passenger turned her blurry eyes in my direction and said, "I'm glad you're not one of those niggers."

I could feel the people in the back-seat cringing. The man said, "Now Claire, maybe the driver doesn't like to hear that kind of language."

"Oh, honey," she said, patting my arm, "You don't mind if I'm honest, do you?"

"I have no problem with your honesty at all," I replied.

"See," she said to her friend in the

back seat. She smiled and batted her false eyelashes at me.

"However," I continued, "I find your bigotry most unbecoming and indicative of a small mind." I wish I had a camera to catch the incredible expression on that face gawking at me. But what was even better were the faces I saw in the rearview mirror. They looked like they were about to explode and were trying heroically not to laugh. Obviously, the dowager in the front seat was someone they feared. I was thoroughly enjoying myself. We reached Chargin's and as I expected, my now silently fuming front seat companion automatically paid the $6.20 fare with exactly six dollars and twenty cents. Then with much drama and annoyance, exited the cab.

As the people in the back climbed out, the man winked, smiled at me and slipped me a 10-dollar bill. Sometimes it's good to be a cab driver.

Chapter 5

It was about 3:30 on a slow Tuesday morning. My unconscious passenger and I were heading east into the Sierra Nevada's. We were about an hour out of Reno. Suddenly my companion stirred. He woke up, groggily looked around, and tentatively asked, "Where are we?"

I told him that we were about an hour away from Reno. This revelation took him by complete surprise. He asked, really bewildered now, "Why are we doing that?"

"Because you wanted to get laid."

"Oh." He considered this for a while, then sort of weakly observed, "Doesn't sound very smart, does it?"

"Well, it certainly isn't the way I'd be spending my money right now," I shot back. He mulled this over for a while, struggled to the conclusion that we were headed in the wrong direction, and finally made the painful decision to turn around.

"Well, you'd better take me home,"

he said with some chagrin.

"And where might that be?" asks I.

"Travis Air Force Base," says he.

It was good to see that his ability to reason was slowly reviving. I wanted to both encourage and reward this sound thinking, so I told him that I wouldn't charge him any more to take him all the way back home. Because Travis Air Force Base was about three hours west of our current position, my newfound friend, John, was touched by my offer and insisted on giving me an extra $40 for my efforts.

I had encountered John around 2 a.m. hitchhiking up J Street in Sacramento. When he saw me he flagged me down. I pulled over, opened the front door for him, and he toppled in.

"I want a woman," he proclaimed.

"You mean to rent?" I inquired.

"Yeah," he said, "I want a hooker."

"Look, pal," I replied, "I wouldn't touch any of the women working these streets with your dick."

"Well, where can I find a decent hooker?" he cried.

I answered that the women working in brothels in Nevada were Grade A, Government Inspected.

"Great," he said, his eyes bright with desire. "Let's go."

And that's how our adventure had begun.

Chapter 6

"Why do you wear those gloves," asked the young woman in the back seat. She had been quiet for most of the ride. Some passengers don't feel much like talking. After a few monosyllabic replies to my verbal entireties followed by silence, I get the message and leave them alone.

"Sometimes I get assaulted and must defend myself," I replied. She became silent again.

After a while we reached her apartment complex. She paid the fare, no tip, but that was okay. I could tell she didn't have a whole lot of money. She reached for the door handle, then stopped and looked at me.

"I was assaulted," she confided. "Six years ago." She proceeded to recount her horrifying ordeal. She related details of how she felt, what she was thinking, and her overpowering sense of helplessness and hopelessness. She had been abducted, beaten, raped, beaten again.

I became engulfed in an unbounded,

blinding rage. I became capable of gleeful murder. If only I had that rapist's cowardly neck in my hands...

I have a well-developed sense of justice that is grievously insulted by stories such as this. All too often I encounter women with fresh bruises and welts. It breaks my heart. There's a price for me to pay as well. The violence that some men visit upon some women makes it harder for any woman to trust any man. Sometimes that barrier is insurmountable. In the more than two decades that my wife, Jackie, and I have been married, I have never even raised a threatening hand to her. I couldn't. It would destroy my self-respect as a man, as a human being. How could I ever look at myself in the mirror again?

I asked her if she had sought counseling. She said in the six years since she had been attacked she had never told anyone. She felt ashamed and responsible. I told her that what she was feeling was typical of many of the women who have experienced sexual assault. I gently but firmly suggested that those feelings were counterproductive and total bullshit. Nothing she could have possibly said or done could justify in any way such inhuman behavior, and that 100 percent of the blame and responsibility rested with the miscreant animal who had done this to her.

We talked for more than an hour. We cried, and we even laughed; I don't remember what it was we laughed about, but I do recall laughing. It was a cathartic experience for both of us. I encouraged her to contact the Women's Center, and possibly get into a support group of women with similar experiences. It was important for her not to feel alone.

When it was time for her to leave, she asked if she could have a hug. I got out of the car and gently wrapped my arms around her. As she clung to me she told me that this was the first time a man had held her since that dreadful night. I didn't know what to say.

Chapter 7

If there is such a thing as reincarnation, I want to come back as one of my wife Jackie's dogs. We have three dogs and live with three cats. You never really own a cat. In the wintertime, they all climb into bed with us. One morning I counted 140 toes in that bed. I imagine there is some piece of legislation, somewhere banning that practice.

The newest arrival to our household is Bingo, a now old Springer Spaniel who moved into the home behind us along with his family. Bingo was never brought inside. He was chained to a tree and his owners never touched him, never talked to him, while they provided him with food, water and shelter (in the form of a dog house) he enjoyed very little social interaction.

This state of affairs nearly killed Jackie, who unfortunately could see Bingo's woeful countenance from our kitchen window and back deck. For more than a year and a half, Jackie implored the people to talk to the dog, touch him, and to take him for walks. Finally, our neighbors, who really were decent people, suggested that if we were so concerned about Bingo's welfare, he could come live with us.

For the past five years, every morning at around 6:45 Bingo is having his coffee and toast in bed with his new mom, two other dogs and three cats while watching the morning news.

Our oldest dog is a miniature black and tan Dachshund named Teeny. We call her "Teeny Weenie." Jackie takes great delight in calling up and down the street for her Teeny Weenie. She determined that this little weenie dog didn't make me look bad enough, so she went out and bought an apricot Toy Poodle, and that little flamer makes me look plenty bad. The poodle is listed in the AKC Registry under the name of Cardinal Richelieu La Grandeur. We call him Little Rickie.

Being of French ancestry, Rickie feels compelled to be annoying, and therefore barks incessantly. To be honest, he has few apparent redeeming qualities. He does, however, have an insidious way of worming his way into your heart. God knows why, but over the years, I have grown quite fond of the little critter.

One Saturday morning around 6:00 I stopped by my house and picked up Little Rickie. He likes going for cab rides. As soon as I got him in the car the dispatcher called for a cab in Rancho. I snatched up my mic and volunteered to go. Rickie and I were soon speeding East on Highway 50.

Ahead of us, the sun proceeded to rise over the high Sierras. It was magnificent, and as it turned out, the image of the rising sun was prophetic: We picked up a Japanese businessman. Who, God love him, wanted to go all the way to the airport. This was a big ride! Rickie is really well behaved in the cab. He doesn't bark, and is friendly to the passengers; if they're not receptive, he leaves them alone. Our current fare enjoyed Rickie's company, and Rickie sat on his lap, receiving pets and scratches all the way to the airport.

When we arrived, our passenger paid the fare and handed me an extra $5. Looking me in the eyes he said, "Tip for you." Then he gave me another $1 bill saying, "Tip for dog." I picked Rickie up and held his back to my chest. As we bowed slightly, I said, "Domo arrigato." Our foreign visitor beamed, returned our bow and walked away.

That's how Little Rickie earned his first dollar.

Chapter 8

I was dropping my first-time passenger, Brad, off at the Graduate Bar in Davis. Mr. Meter said "32 bucks." He handed me three twenties and told me to keep the change. Swiftly, I gave him my card and asked him to call me when he needed a ride out of there. Around 11:45 my phone rang, it was Brad, he wanted another ride. Luckily, I was just dropping off in West Sac. and had no other rides pending. I told him that I'd be there by midnight. Brad was waiting outside the bar when I arrived. He had hooked up with a drop-dead beautiful woman. She had red hair, green eyes and a body that defied gravity. She taught astrophysics at U.C. Davis, a feast for the eyes and a feast for the mind!

We drove towards Sacramento, as we crossed the Yolo Causeway, Brad said they were headed to the Zebra Club at 19th and P. Sheila asked if they could go to the Pine Cove instead. Brad insisted that he really wanted to see Dave, the bartender at the Zebra, but Sheila still wanted to go to the Pine

Cove. They were clearly at an impasse. "We could be in Tahoe by 2:30," I interjected. I was just trying to be helpful. They looked at each other, smiled and enthusiastically said, "OK, let's do that!!" We stopped at the Tower Bottle Shop at 16th and Broadway where Brad purchased two bottles of Dom Perignon for the ride to the lake.

These two were married, but not to each other. They had been high school sweethearts but had never consummated their relationship (so to speak.) These years they had wondered about one another, what would it have been like? Well, after consuming two bottles of Champaign and hearing numerous romantic and passionate poems delivered by yours truly, they found out. Right in the back seat of my cab!!

Beyond this place there be dragons!

Chapter 9

It was about 2:30 on a deadly dull Sunday morning. I was catching a nap in front of the yet-to-be completed Hyatt. Asleep though I might have been, I still had an ear cocked and thus was somewhat aware of at least my audio environment. I heard voices and then footsteps. By the time the two rather large men reached the cab, I was awake and fully alert.

"We want to go to the South area, but we want to pick up some bitches on the way," said one of the two men. They were young and black; I am neither.

"I don't give a flying fuck where you want to go, Pal, as long as I get paid when we get there," I shot back.

"Hell, man, I'll pay you right now," he said, waving a couple 20s in my direction.

"There's no need for that," I said, unlocking the doors. "Welcome aboard, Gents."

When I look at a passenger, I don't see white, black, red, yellow or brown. I see green. I want to provide a service for which I am fairly paid. Anyone who gets in my cab regardless of their race gets treated the way I would want to be treated myself. Most of the black folks who ride with me take notice of the environment I create, and seem to relax and even enjoy themselves. My current adventure would not prove to be so enjoyable.

I look like such an old redneck that I've developed a strategy for dealing with young black kids. As soon as we are on our way, I offer everyone a piece of Doublemint gum. Before they got in the car I would already have punched in FM 102, one of the local rap stations, on the radio and now I would crank it up. Then I'd drive like an asshole (don't forget, these are deserted streets). Within minutes, the kids usually love me. Some of them have taken to calling me "Cool Breeze."

These young fellows and I were having a really good time. We swung through Oak Park and the lusty lads connected up with some of the local talent drifting up and down Broadway. One of the girls jumped up front with me. We proceeded down to G Parkway, an after-hours "Business District" in the South area. We pulled up in front of a rock house to purchase recreational supplies.

The two men got out of the cab and went into the house. I turned off the lights, kept the engine running with the car in drive, and my foot on the brake. I set the mirrors so that I could see 180 degrees behind me and continually scanned the scene both in front and to the rear. A rock house is a very busy place. People are constantly coming and going, and some people are just hanging around, hoping to score for some of the customers while breaking off a piece for themselves.

One of the guys hanging around was checking me out. After a while, he went inside and not long afterwards my passengers returned along with some of the folks from the house. One of them sticks his face in the car, looks at me hard for a moment, and says, "Oh, yeah, you're Task Force."

Now he stands up and yells at the two guys I brought, "You get the fuck outta here and don't you ever show up here again with the POLice!" It was quite apparent that the young men had been sampling the goods, as both were speeding pretty heavily. I realized my situation had become quite precarious. If you are a cocaine smoker, once you've taken that first hit off of the pipe, all you can think of is more. If a user does not get more cocaine, he starts to crave it and can think of nothing else. A person in this condition is said to be "fiending." It is at this time that the cocaine smoker is the most dangerous. There is nothing they won't do to get more.

I have seen people do horrible, scandalous things to each other and to themselves to get more. Eight out of ten violent crimes in California are committed by people who want more. Now I found myself driving down the road with two most likely heavily armed fiending pipe-heads sitting right behind me who were incredibly pissed off. They had willing women and plenty of money, but no drugs because everybody was convinced that I was a cop. Mine was not an enviable position. From time to time I find myself in situations that prompt me to ask, "Am I going to get out of this one alive?" I really hate those times when the answer is in doubt. This was just such a time.

The guy directly behind me started screaming about how much he hated cops. Suddenly I heard the slide of an automatic being pulled back as a round was chambered. Then my enraged passenger stuck the gun's barrel to the back of my head. He whispered in my ear, but loud enough for everyone to hear, "I'm gonna blow you away just on general principals. What do you think of that, Mr. Cabman?" He was toying with his prey.

At this point, my instincts took over and I was seized by a blinding rage. "You can think I'm a cop. You can bust a cap into my head. Nothing I can do will stop you. BUT I’M SURE AS FUCK NOT GOING TO BEG YOU ASSHOLES!" I bellowed the last sentence at the top of my lungs.

There was a stunned, dead silence in the car. I glanced at the woman sitting up front with me. Her mouth had dropped open and her eyes were bulging wide. Under different circumstances, her expression would be humorous. Humor was definitely not one of the emotions I was currently experiencing. I do remember rather calmly wondering if I would be able to see my brains on the inside of the windshield before losing consciousness. The things that go through one's mind at such times...

The eternal oppressive silence was finally broken by a chuckling sound, accompanied by the removal of the gun from the back of my head. "You're pretty tough, Mr. Cabman," said my would-be murderer. "Pull over here."

I immediately complied, and as they were all piling out of the cab, the gunman threw a $20 bill at me. There was $32 on the meter, but I didn't feel like pushing my luck. As I drove back to the Hyatt, I tried to figure out why I was still alive. I concluded that had I pleaded for my life, I would have undoubtedly been killed. My defiance in the face of death gave my assailants something to respect, and I was able to pierce the effects of the drugs and speak to whatever humanity still resided in their souls.

I never did tell, my wife, Jackie

about this little incident.

Chapter 10

It was about 4:30 on a chilly April morning. I was picking up a male guest at the Rio Consumnes Correctional Center, the Sacramento Sheriff's South County Detention facility. We have a contract with the Sheriff and haul his released inmates to the jail or courthouse nearest to the location at which they were arrested. The county pays for that part of the ride; any further transportation costs must be paid by the passenger/former inmate.

I had been inside the office where a pretty female deputy signed my charge slip. I like lady cops. I've always been attracted to heavily armed women, but that's another story. My passenger was being released from the lockup and was hurrying towards the cab. He was wearing a pair of shorts and suspenders. Period. No shirt, shoes, or socks. By the time he jumped into the front seat, he was shaking with the cold. I revved up the heater and in a while he stopped trembling.

The Sheriff was paying for this lad's ride to Isleton, a sleepy community on the Sacramento River, somewhere between Walnut Grove and Rio Vista. I think you get the picture. The man next to me was about 25. From what he was wearing, it was easy to see that he was trim. He had long, jet-black hair. He was from Chile, spoke English well, and was very polite.

I asked him where he needed to go. He said that he lived at Owl Harbor on Brannon Island, about 5 miles south of Isleton. I explained that any ride beyond Isleton was on him. He said the money was no problem, except for the fact that he'd have to swim across the river to get it once we arrived there. This was certainly an interesting development, I'm thinking to myself. What are the odds of this guy swimming across that very cold river three times just to get me paid?

There would be no place open in Isleton this time of the morning, so I decided to take a chance on this likable young man. We finally arrived at Owl Harbor around 5:15 a.m. We walked to the end of a pier and my passenger, Carlos, pointed towards a houseboat some 300 yards across the slough and said that his money was there. He held up the pointer finger of his right hand. Smiling and nodding he uttered those famous last words, "I'll be right back."

Without further ado, he plunged into the water and swam towards the distant houseboat. Oh, God, I wish he hadn't said that! That's usually the last thing a cabbie hears when somebody's trying to run out on them. Those words make cabdrivers cringe. Believe me, it's worse than fingernails being slowly scratched down a blackboard. I watched Carlos make his way across the slough and thought to myself; I should just leave right now. He's not coming back. Hell, I wouldn't come back. But I wanted to see how it would turn out.

After what seemed to be a long time, and it's a safe bet it seemed even longer to Carlos, he hauled himself onto the deck of the houseboat. He stood up, held aloft his right pointer finger, gesturing "One minute," and disappeared inside. Again, my doubts were running rampant. But soon my soggy friend reappeared, folded a piece of paper, clenched it in his teeth, and God love him, plunged back into that cold, cold water.

He finally arrived with a $20 bill clenched in his chattering teeth. The fare was $10, so I folded two five's the same way and gave them to him. I reached over and shook his hand and thanked him from the bottom of my heart for his honesty. I watched Carlos make the last leg of his watery journey to be sure that he completed it safely. Once again he pulled himself onto the houseboat's deck. He stood and looked in my direction. Seeing me, he waved. I took off my hat and made long sweeping arcs with it in a final attempt to convey my appreciation for, and admiration of what I had just witnessed.

The ride back to Sacramento was beautiful. The sky was crystal clear and a remarkable shade of blue. There was a crimson band over the eastern horizon, all of which was reflected on the numerous waterways that covered the landscape. Once again, my belief in the fundamental goodness of human beings had been resoundingly reaffirmed. The thought occurred to me that I probably should have taken him that last five miles for free, but then this would not have been as good a story.

Chapter 11

It was about 5 a.m. I rolled up on the Texas Saloon, a krankster/biker/pool hall/bar that stays open after hours and serves coffee. My fare was standing outside waiting for his cab. He was a tall man, expensive suit, in his mid-30s, and he was profoundly twisted. I opened the front door for him. After he settled in and told me where to go, he looked at me with his bleary eyes and slurred the words, "Tell me not in mournful numbers."

I must admit this caught me by surprise. My newfound friend had uttered the opening words from a poem by Longfellow. My surprise, however, paled in comparison to his look of shock and disbelief when I shot back, "That life is but an empty dream?" which happens to be the second line of this not-so-well-known poem. We traded lines until the poem was finished and each of us savored the specialness of the moment.

To me the essence of art is to feel something inside and to use whatever your medium is to reach out and touch that same something in someone else's inside. When that touching happens, it is art and it is magic. To feel that magic is life affirming. This is, I believe, one of the reasons we are alive -- To create and to enjoy art.

So, my passenger (whose name was Phil) and I drove through the early morning darkness reciting our favorite poems. He really got pissed off when he realized that I knew more poetry than did he.

"It's not fair! It's not right!" He was upset because He was a successful lawyer who earned six figures a year. He had original art on his walls and he had Dali and Picasso prints. He had autographed first edition books by well-known authors in his library and it blew him out that I, a lowly cabdriver, had committed more poetry to memory than he had.

We had worked our way through Longfellow, Yates, Frost, Cummings, Coleridge, Dunne, Sandburg, and some of my stuff when he ran out. At this point I asked him if he was up for hearing "The Raven." He refused to believe that I had memorized that particular work. When I was a truck driver I had concluded that the brain, like any other muscle, would atrophy if not used. Therefore, in order to avoid a withered, shriveled brain, I decided to memorize Edgar Allan Poe's "The Raven" and once having done so, I have recited it every morning for the last 20 years. I believe it is my mantra. I unscrupulously took advantage of this situation by suggesting that we make a small wager, say $100. He greedily jumped at my offer.

I proceeded to deliver upon him a word perfect, no holds barred, petal to the metal, small craft-warning recital of "The Raven." Phil had been, in the words of my wife Jackie, "ravened." She is convinced that I have turned the word raven into a verb. She further contends that anyone who has been ravened will never be quite the same. I must admit that Phil's eyes became even more glazed, but when he was finally able to speak, he said that I had blown his socks off and gladly paid the bet.

Chapter 12

I had dropped some folks off at an apartment complex near the Sacramento River. It was about 2:30 on a Wednesday morning. Just after I turned onto the Garden Highway, I saw an owl flash into the beam of my headlights. Before I could even begin to react, I hit the bird. The collision threw him over the car. I stopped and backed up to where he lay on his back, wings quivering. I got out of the car, picked him up, and set him down on his feet at the side of the road. He stood there with his right wing hanging down and slowly rocked back and forth. His eyes were glazed and I could almost see the little cartoon stars and birdies circling above his head.

I knew that if I left him there he would probably die, either by stumbling into traffic, becoming prey for some predator, or probably worst of all by starving. I had no choice. I loaded the bird into the front seat and took off at high speed for U.C. Davis. There was a vet-med teaching hospital on the campus that operated a

24-hour emergency clinic for injured and/or sick critters.

About half an hour later we arrived. I announced over the after-hours intercom by the locked front door that I had an injured owl. I was instructed to bring him in. We were ushered into a treatment room, were told that the on-call vet would arrive soon, and were left alone. There I sat with what turned out to be a male Great Horned Owl, over a foot and a half tall. He was perched on my left hand. Luckily, I was wearing my leather gloves. Our faces were less than a foot away from each other. I was captivated by his eyes. They were huge, perfectly round, with yellow irises and large black pupils. I was surprised by the almost feline quality of those magnificent orbs.

We stared at each other for what seemed to be a very long time. I tried to think soothing and supportive thoughts. I kept silent, fearing that the sound of a human voice might alarm my new injured friend. So we sat there, silently communing and gazing into each other's eyes. Yes, sir, we were spending quality time together. Here I was bonding with a very large owl. Finally, the vet came in and closed the door. I tried to pass the bird over to her, but he flew across the room. The very surprised, and somewhat shaken vet said she was amazed that such a large bird, well enough to fly, hadn't torn me into very little pieces. She told me of the time she saw a bird that size dig its talons into a man's arm all the way to the bone. They had to anesthetize the bird in order to get it to release its grip.

Gosh, I thought to myself. That sounded like a whole lot of fun! I'm sure that I wasn't spared injury because of any affection this bird may have developed for me. Most likely I wasn't ripped to shreds only because the thought had yet to pass through his still shaken mind. I have no doubt the idea would have eventually occurred to him. I left my feathered friend in the capable hands of the vet and returned to Sacramento to try to make some money in what was left of my morning.

I kept in touch with the people at UCD. The bird was lucky. He had a bump on his head and a bruised wing and was healthy after about a month.

He was released into the wild, not far from the location of our first encounter.

Chapter 13

I pulled up to the Heritage Inn in Rancho Cordova on Point East Drive at nearly 4 A.M. It had taken me the better part of 20 minutes to get there. As I hit the driveway, a figure appeared out of nowhere and jumped into the front seat after I opened the door.

"Take me to Elk Grove," he said quickly. My heart skipped a beat. It had been a particularly gruesome night. No-goes and dinkers and damn few of those. The Eighth Amendment to the U.S. Constitution prohibits cruel and unusual punishment. This night was stomping all over my rights as guaranteed by that particular Amendment. But now, everything was just fine. This one ride would save my bacon. I was turning onto Folsom Boulevard thinking about how great it was to be a cab driver and how even the most dismal of nights can be turned around right out of the blue. It was then that I noticed the angry hive of Sheriffs' vehicles swarming around the intersection of Folsom and Sunrise, which was now directly ahead of us. Suddenly they all lit up their red and blue lights and made a mad dash for my cab. Other elements of the posse appeared to my rear also illuminating the night with those red and blue flashing lights. I stopped dead right where I was and held my hands against the windshield so they could be easily seen. Sheriffs' cars came to screeching halts all around us. Doors flew open and what seemed like a small army of deputies came rushing headlong at my cab, its hapless driver and passenger. They were chambering rounds into the shotguns most of them were carrying and continued to thunder towards us. I figured they probably weren't after me. This just isn't the way they respond to a California rolling stop, not even in Rancho Cordova. Sure enough, they ran to my passenger's door, threw it open, and dragged him out. I got out myself and asked one of the deputies what my passenger was supposed to have done. The young officer said that he had robbed one of the hotels on Point East Drive.

"Does this mean I don't get to take him to Elk Grove?" I asked, crestfallen.

"I'm afraid not." was the chuckled reply. Just then they were removing a rather large handgun from under the jacket of my already handcuffed, would be long distance passenger.

"How much does he owe you?" the deputy asked. I checked the meter and said, "He's into me for $2.80, but under the circumstances I guess I'll just have to eat it."

The now somewhat sympathetic cop said, "No! He owes it to you. Let's get you paid."

We went over to the prisoner. "Hey, you owe the cabbie $2.80."

"My money is in my wallet." was the reply. They pulled some money out of the wallet.

"Give him a fiver. Tell him to keep the change," my former passenger said.

As I was returning to Sacramento, disappointed, alone, and still having a bad night, I thought about the desperado I had left behind. It was obvious that he wasn't going to grow up to be a rocket scientist. What kind of idiot pulls an armed robbery and then calls a cab? The get-a-way is one of the more important elements to this type of activity. The guy couldn't have been all bad I concluded. Even under such dire circumstances he still thought to give me a tip. Every time I think I've seen it all...

Chapter 14

I guess some lessons you have to learn the hard way. When I first started to drive cabs, I would let the passengers sit wherever they wished.

One night a young man got into the back seat directly behind me. We hadn't gone very far when he told me to pull over and proceeded to slug me in the back of my head. I went down on the seat. He got out of the car and went to the driver's door. I played possum and stayed still. When he reached the front door I took hold of the steering wheel with my right hand and yanked myself upright and at the same time I threw open the door with my left arm. I used every ounce of strength I could muster. My efforts were rewarded with a very satisfying thud as the door caught my assailant squarely in the mid and upper torso. The thud was immediately followed by an "oouff" as air involuntarily exploded from his lungs. He staggered back. I piled out of the cab, grabbed him by the back of his collar and hit him with a building for a while. Then I hit him with the sidewalk. Although he remained conscious, he made no effort to get up. I was hoping that he would consider this an educational experience. Probably not.

My guess was that he was a "fiender," someone who has recently run out of rock cocaine and will do anything to get more. These people are highly motivated for money and operate in an ethical vacuum. I am afraid the only lesson this dip shit learned was to use a gun next time. I informed the dispatcher about the attempted robbery and told him that the attemptee probably needed medical assistance.

Within two minutes I heard sirens. A Sac P.D. unit all lit up and siren blaring came wheeling around the corner of 10th and J Streets and screeched to a halt. A young cop came flying out of his car and appraised the situation.

"I'm the cab driver," I volunteered helpfully. "This solid citizen tried to rob me," I said, pointing to my former passenger, who was now kissing the sidewalk. I showed the officer the knot on my head. He looked down at the young man, whose face was a real mess. Then he looked back up at me. Our eyes met, and after a moment or two he said, "I guess this guy fell down." I replied, "Yes, I tried to catch him, but I missed."

They took him to the hospital, where it was determined that he had a broken nose and a fractured skull. And then they took him to jail. Ever since that night I will not let a male passenger riding alone with me sit in the back seat.

Chapter 15

I was headed east on Highway 50 for a 5:30 a.m. time call in Rosemont. At this time of morning a call in this area is likely to go to the airport. I arrived at the address ten minutes early. It was a nice house in a nice neighborhood. Yes sir, this really smelled like a trip to the airport, which would round out my shift very nicely.

The lady who opened the door appeared to be in her late 50's or early 60's. Her clothes looked expensive, but were badly rumpled. Her hair, which she wore up, was in disarray, as was her make-up. The house was furnished with expensive, although dated furniture, and had obviously been neglected for a long time. There was a faint aroma of urine. She asked me to help her with some bags, pointing to the dining room table upon which sat two paper shopping bags. Clearly this trip wasn't going to the airport, but perhaps it would still be a long trip.

"I'd like to go to the nearest

motel," the lady said, once again dashing my hopes.

"That would be the Howard Johnson's," I said (which was about half a mile away).

"I don't need anything that fancy," she snapped. I suggested the Sierra View on Folsom Boulevard, which would be $5 away. She said the Sierra View would be fine.

I grabbed the bags and headed for the door. She asked if she could hold on to my elbow. It was then that I noticed that the lady was blind. I touched her hand with my elbow and she latched on. I guided her through the front door, which she didn't bother to lock and out to the cab. She asked to ride up front. She was pulling out a cigarette as we were pulling out of the driveway and said rather nastily, "I suppose you won't let me smoke in here."

"Please, be my guest. Knock yourself out," was my gracious reply. I whipped out my trusty Zippo and lit her Virginia Slim. I used to be very militant about people smoking around me, becoming righteously indignant about them assaulting me with the noxious by-product of their neurotic habit. Well I certainly sold out on that one. Trustee Zippo indeed.

The lady took a drag off her cigarette and turned her sightless eyes towards me.

"How come you're not being a shit?" she asked, still with an edge of belligerence.

"Hey," I said, "Give me a chance. We just met. I'm sure once you get to know me you won't like me at all."

This particular feeble attempt at humor hit its mark with a vengeance. First, she laughed in spite of herself, and then she laughed uncontrollably and contagiously. Here I was laughing my head off with the lady who was ruining my morning. But laugh we did. We both had tears in our eyes from laughing. She reached out, touched my shoulder, and thanked me for the laugh. Apparently, it had been a long time since her last one. That's a shame, I thought. I believe laughter is a very important part of life. It can be therapeutic, cathartic, and hell, it's just plain fun. This was back when we were dispatched by radio. I regained my composure enough to check in with Yvonne, the dispatcher on duty that morning. I informed her I would be clearing in Rosemont SHORTLY. "Great," she said. "There's a 6 a.m. time call in the town of Folsom." My morning salvation had arrived. From the ashes of Rosemont arose the beautiful phoenix carrying me to Folsom for yet another shot at an airport trip. It would be tight getting to Folsom in time, but we were just arriving at the Sierra View and once I popped current passenger off, if I hurried I could just make it.

"Could you help me register and make sure that I get into the room okay?" she asked. So much for making it to Folsom on time.

"Sure," I said. Inwardly I was eating my liver, but I resolved to give this woman, my passenger, the time and the attention she deserved. We went into the office and I filled out the registration form. She paid for the room and I made sure she received the correct change. We drove to Room 105. Carrying her bags, I guided her through the door and got her settled in her room. She pulled a bill from her wallet and asked its denomination. One last test.

"That's a twenty," I said.

"I want you to have it," she said, offering it to me. And then she thanked me for being so very kind. I thanked her for the generous tip and told her it was a pleasure having her on board. As I left, the last thing I said was, "Thanks for calling Yellow."

Although I didn't make it to Folsom by 6 a.m., I did get the gentleman to the airport in plenty of time to catch his plane.

Around 12:30 that afternoon I was awakened from a dead sleep by a phone call from a Sacramento County Sheriff deputy. He asked if I had picked up a lady in Rosemont around 5:30 that morning. I replied affirmatively. He asked where I took her. I asked why he wanted to know. I consider confidentiality an important part of my service, and I don't violate my passenger's privacy without good reason.

"Her social worker believes she may be attempting to take her life."

"She checked into the Sierra View Motel, 9200 Folsom Boulevard, Room 105," I said without further hesitation.

Later that night I stopped by the Sierra View and found out that the lady had indeed checked out permanently. I was glad that we shared that wonderful laugh. I was glad that her last direct human encounter was a gentle one. I keep pondering the idea that the last words she heard may have been "Thanks for calling Yellow."

Chapter 16

I was the second cab in line at Cal Expo. It was the fifth day of the State Fair. The car in front of me was also a Yellow cab. The driver was new, young, and black. I had yet to meet him, but he was sitting there when I arrived a couple of minutes before. We were the only two cabs in the lineup. Etiquette in Cabland dictates that the first cab on the scene should be the first one to load up. A guy came out of the fair, passed up the first cab and came directly to my car. As he got in I explained that the fellow in front of me had been waiting longer and really deserved the trip more than I did.

"Yeah, but you're white," said my wannabe passenger.

"Oh," I said pleasantly, "You don't ride with black folks, huh?"

"Nope," he replied, "I hate niggers."

"Yeah? Well I hate bigots. Now get

the fuck out of my cab."

Chapter 17

We arrived at the apartment complex by 49th Avenue and Franklin Boulevard. The young man I had transported from Sutterville Road smiled and said "I can hook you up with anything you want. You want powder? You want rock? You want bitches? You want bud? Anything you want."

"You can hook me up with anything?" I asked, an expectant smile on my face.

"Yeah, anything you want," he said, with an even bigger smile on his face.

"Well then, how 'bout hooking me up with the 7 dollars you owe me for this ride?" I said, pointing to the meter and no longer smiling. The smile disappeared from his face as well.

"Oh, man, I ain't got no cash," was his plaintive reply.

"The time to discuss alternate forms of payment is at the beginning of the ride, not at the end," I explained. "Now that you've had your cab ride and I'm not getting paid, I feel like a chump. You don't want me to feel like a chump, do you?" I asked, putting my face in his. He cringed.

"No... No, I guess not," was his weak reply.

"Trust me, it would not bode well for your continued good health," I pointed out.

"So, what are we going to do? I honestly don't have any money," he bleated.

"Well, in that case, we're going to take another cab ride back in the direction from which we came. Only a little further. If you make a move for that door handle, I promise you that you will need a ride in an ambulance. Are you catching my drift here?" I asked, staring intently into his eyes.

"Yes, sir," he said with resignation.

I took him all the way down to Cal-Expo, some 5 miles beyond the point of our initial encounter.

Chapter 18

"For God's sakes, please don't shoot me," he whimpered loudly. His eyes were crazed. He was sitting up front with me and was cowering against the door.

I had picked him up at a South area bar and for some reason the barkeep and all of the patrons seemed very happy to see me arrive. I heard an audible sigh of relief as my new buddy and I headed out the door towards the cab.

"Hey, I don't want to shoot you." I replied in a calming voice. "I just want to get you home." I fixed my eyes on his and continued with a somewhat firmer tone, "Now tell me where you live."

"By Florin and Greenhaven," he blurted out. We headed in that direction.

I told the dispatcher where and when we would be landing.

"Great," Tamara said, "There's a 10 o'clock time call holding down there.

Let me know when you're clear." Tamara has such a sweet voice that people actually look at the radio when she talks, and working with her is a genuine joy.

Perfect! A 10 o'clock time call. This could be an airport shot! It was now 9:40 p.m., so I had just enough time to drop this guy off and make the pick-up on time. I headed towards Greenhaven and Florin. I realized there was no point in trying to carry on a normal conversation with my paranoid passenger. Whatever substance he had been abusing, combined with fear and was eating what was left of his brain. I gratefully settled for his silence as he continued to cower in the corner. He never took his crazed eyes off of me. I had my stun gun ready. It was not one of my more enjoyable cab rides.

After what seemed to be an eternity (in reality only about ten minutes) we arrived at Florin and Greenhaven.

"Alright," I said, "Where should I pull over?" He looked around and pointed to a corner house.

"Pull in the driveway," he

requested. I turned into the driveway.

Now came one of the more fun situations a cab drive must endure. There are people expecting you to pick them up at a specific time (which was rapidly approaching) and now I'm dealing with some crazed asshole who doesn't have a clue about what's going on. I looked at the meter. It read $12.40.

"You owe me twelve bucks," I said.

"What?" he replied without a trace of comprehension. I decided to make this as simple and clear as possible. Once again, I fixed his eyes with mine and stuck my face a little closer to his.

"You owe me twelve dollars for this cab ride. I want my money now," I said, placing great emphasis on the word 'now.' This time the message got through, and he reached into the right pocket of his jeans and produced a tightly crumpled piece of paper, which was obviously money. He gave it to me. I uncrumpled it and, of course, found it to be a $1 bill.

He was looking at me for further

instructions.

"More money," I said, trying to keep the message simple. He nodded and once again reached into his pocket and produced -- you guessed it -- another crumpled $1 bill.

Why? Why, God, do you place such idiots on this earth to plague me? We repeated our amusing little routine another five times. It was a good thing I didn't have a gun because shooting this jerk seemed like an increasingly good idea, and I have every confidence that it would have vastly improved the gene pool. The eighth crumpled up bill he gave me was a $100. I had $35 cash on me, including my change wad.

"Hey, I can't even come close to changing that! What else do you have?" Time was marching on. The seasons seemed to be changing as I sat there in this nightmare situation. He once again reached into his pocket. This time he pulled out the lining. The well was dry.

I had neither the time nor the inclination to continue with this search.

"Okay," I said. "I'll settle for the 7 bucks." I held out the $100 bill for him.

"No!" he screamed. "Keep it!" He grabbed the door handle, and before I could shove the bill in his shirt pocket, he was gone. He had run around the corner and by the time I backed out of the driveway and rounded the corner myself, he was nowhere in sight.

I was five minutes late for my 10 o'clock time call, who had mercifully given themselves plenty of time to catch their 11:15 Amtrak train. The people enjoyed my explanation for being tardy so much that they gave me an extra big tip.

Chapter 19

I met Marcia Mars just as the sun was setting. It was 8:30 on a late June evening. The light was soft and the shadows were long. I picked up Marcia at Mercy General Hospital. She appeared to be in her late 60's or early 70's. She had a quick mind, a well-developed sense of humor, and a worldly, classically educated air about her. We were thoroughly enjoying the falling night, the ride, and the company. A Chopin ballad was softly playing on the radio. I recited The Tale of the Wandering Angus, by William Butler Yates. It's a wonderfully romantic poem that seems to deeply touch many people who encounter it.

I walked out to the hazel woods

Because a fire was in my head

I cut and peeled a hazel wand

And tied a berry to a thread.

When white moths were on the wing

And moth like stars were flickering out

I dropped the berry in a stream

And I caught a little silver trout.

When I had laid it on the floor

And bent to blow the fire aflame

I heard a rustling on the floor

And someone called me by my name.

It had become a glimmering girl

With apple blossom in her hair

Who called me by my name

And ran and faded through

Brightening air.

Now I am old with wandering

Through hollow lands

And hilly lands

But I'll find out

Where she has gone

And kiss her lips

And take her hands

And we will walk among

Long dappled grass

And pluck till time

And times are done

The silver apples of the moon

The golden apples of the sun

When we arrived at her house in a very nice neighborhood, she wrote me a check with a generous tip. She asked my name and I told her Solitske.

"It's Irish," I said, "We shortened it. It used to be O'Solitske." Another one of my feeble attempts at humor.

About two years later I had a call for a patient at Mercy General ER. No name was given. I walked into the emergency room and was directed to Treatment Room 5, where I found Marcia Mars, who I hadn't seen since our first encounter.

She looked up and her eyes brightened.

"Good evening, Mr. O'Solitske," she said, with a still engaging smile. She had grown frailer, and had started to go downhill. The hospital paid for her ride back to the convalescent home at which she now resided. A conservator had been appointed to administer her finances and she was thoroughly miserable. I shared some poetry with her and I could tell as we rode through the night that for a while at least, she was able to escape the harsh reality of what her life had become.

Maybe six months later I was sitting in front of the Hyatt at about 4 o'clock on a bitterly cold January morning when a bag lady wandered by. She nodded and said Good Morning. I smiled and said "Good morning to you." After she passed and had walked perhaps half a block down L Street I suddenly was able to remember where I had seen that face before. She was Marcia Mars. I slowly drove next to her as she walked and called through the open window.

"Marcia?"

She said, "Yes, hello Mr. O'Solitske." I opened the door and said, "Please get in."

"I have no money for cab rides," was her reply.

"That's not a problem, please get in."

She sat in the front seat. I rolled up the windows and I turned up the heat. I asked where she was going.

"To Denny's, at 3rd and J," was her reply.

When we arrived, I said very carefully, "Marcia, please don't be offended. But do you have any money?"

"No," was her somewhat embarrassed reply.

I gave her $10 so she could get something to eat and stay warm in the restaurant until the sun came up. She took the money, reached out, and touched my cheek with those cold bony fingers, slowly shaking her head. With her eyes fixed on mine, she said, "Nobody does Yates like you do."

Chapter 20

"Need a car in Rancho," said the dispatcher, breaking 45 minutes of silence.

"ELEVEN! ELEVEN! ELEVEN!" I shouted at the top of my lungs into the microphone I was already holding to my lips. When the dispatcher called for a volunteer, if yours was the first number heard, you got the call. Before we went to computer dispatch, the volume of my voice and my quickness sent me on more volunteer calls than any other night driver. It was a matter of reflex and concentration.

My passenger was waiting for me at the Sheraton Hotel on Point East Drive. It was 3 A.M. and for some reason the young lady I picked up wanted to buy a pair of pantyhose. I suggested the Arco AM/PM Minimart just over Highway 50 on Sunrise Boulevard. The round trip would be about $4 on the meter.

"Aren't you going to whine at me about dragging you all this way for such a short trip?" she asked, obviously having dealt with cab drivers before.

"Trust me," I replied. "There's absolutely nothing else going on in Cabland right now, and who knows, I might run into something good out in this neck of the woods."

We arrived at the all-night gas station/market. She got out and made her purchase. When she returned to the cab we headed back to her hotel.

"How much would you charge to take me to Lake Tahoe?" she asked.

"150 dollars," I answered, thinking she was just making small talk.

"Alright, it's a deal," she said, much to my surprise and delight. "Let's swing by my room and pick up my suitcase."

As there was no bellboy on duty, she asked me to come up and help her with her bag. I accompanied her to her suite, where we talked as she packed. She had a great sense of humor and a keen intellect. We immediately developed a good rapport. I could tell she had been drinking, but she was far from twisted. Done with the packing, we headed downstairs. I carried her suitcase, she carried a pillow. I put her case in the trunk and she asked if she could ride up front.

"Sure," I said, "I promise not to bite unless requested."

"We'll have to see about that," was her good-natured reply.

As soon as she got in, she proceeded to put the pillow on my lap, then her head on the pillow.

Just think, I thought to myself, I get paid for doing this. I asked her if she liked poetry.

"No," she said, "I don't like poetry. I love it."

It was as if I had died and gone to Cab Driver's Heaven. Here I was, escaping a deadly dull night in Sacramento, heading into the Sierras with a wonderful lady who loved poetry.

I started off with Yates. As I recited the poem, she moaned and actually started to writhe. It was almost as if my words were physically touching -- no caressing -- her. As we left the lights of Sacramento and Folsom behind, a magical array of stars appeared in the crystalline sky. A dazzling crescent moon almost touching a brilliant Venus rose in the still, blue-black of the eastern horizon. I brought forth into this environment a steady stream of rich, melodic, romantically erotic, rhythmically rhyming words. I could almost see them flow from my mouth into her ear and could actually feel the physical impact they were having upon her.

There's a love within me

That refuses to die

I want to lock it away

But it matters not

How hard I try

The flame is still burning

To say it's not

Would be a lie

But why should I want

My love to hide

How? How? Can I keep

These feelings inside?

I might just as well set out

To turn back the tide

As to try to stop dreaming

Of having you by my side

If it so happens

Our lives can't be shared

I'll remember that once

You may have cared

And if we should have to part

There will always be

A special, special place

For you in my heart

When I concluded, she gave an almost post-orgasmic sigh.

"Oh my God," she gasped unsteadily, "That felt soooo good." We were both short of breath. Our souls, our very beings, connected in an electrifying way. The experience was sensual rather than sexual, intimate rather than carnal, and more profoundly moving than some physical encounters I have had. Damn, talk about safe sex! I am sure both of us were furiously producing endorphins, those psychotropic agents naturally made by the body, which stimulate the brain's pleasure centers like heroin, morphine, and cocaine can only dream of.

We continued on our magical journey. We gazed at the crescent moon and its gemlike companion blazing in the now cobalt-blue Sierra sky. She reached up and caressed my left cheek with her right hand.

"I have a room in Tahoe. Would you like to stay with me?" she asked.

"No, I would not like to stay with you. I would love to stay with you. But I can't I'm a gratefully married man. I love my wife. I just don't do that. But thank you, from the bottom of my heart, for asking."

She continued her observation of the celestial spectacular unfolding in front of us. I showered her with the words of a cab-driving poet. All too soon we rounded Echo Summit. Lake Tahoe lay sparkling under the crimson of the pre-dawn sky. It was magnificent. She asked for a piece of paper and to use my pen. We stopped by the main entrance to Harrah's Hotel & Casino. When we got out she paid the fare, including a generous tip, and gave me a folded piece of paper.

"I wrote this for you."

I unfolded the paper and read aloud:

Does everything as wonderful as the moon

Have to be so very far away?

To my knowledge, I had never before

inspired poetry. I was deeply moved. She kissed my cheek, gave me a sad, sweet, affectionate hug, and walked through the hotel door. As I watched her disappear, it occurred to me that I didn't even know her name.

Chapter 21

It was about 12:30 on a rainy Sunday morning. I picked up a young couple with a brand-new baby. The father was from Pakistan; his wife was a blond American. Her parents were with them. The young Pakistani was very drunk and did not say anything, but the rest of us were having a really good time as we chomped on our Doublemint. I like talking to people from other lands, so I asked the new father, sitting in the back seat, if he was from Karachi.

"No, I am from Lahore!" he hissed, "And if you weren't so ignorant, you would know."

"Look, pal," I said, "I was just trying to include you in the conversation. There's no need to get hostile."

"You just shut your mouth and drive," was his less than cordial reply.

Prior to driving a Yellow cab, I sold computers to doctors. I made really good money, but found myself being nice to some people I didn't particularly like. Believe it or not some doctors can be arrogant, unreasonable and seem to be highly susceptible to cranial rectal inversions. If you're placing a large computer system in a doctor's office the commission can be a sizeable chunk of change. Some doctors feel this gives them the right to really work you over. I realized that in some cases I was selling my self-respect as well as digital systems. After much soul searching I came to the conclusion that standard of living and quality of life are not synonymous terms.

Driving a cab, I never have to be nice to anyone. Given the opportunity I will be nice, and I genuinely enjoy most of the people I haul around. Over the years, after transporting thousands of passengers people from up and down the social-economic spectrum, I must say that my belief in the fundamental goodness of human beings has been (with a few notable exceptions) resoundingly reaffirmed. All I require of my passengers is that they pay for the ride and that they maintain their civility. They don't have to be nice, charming, courteous, cordial, or even smell that great, simply civil.

Every once in a while, -- actually quite rarely, -- I encounter passengers for whom maintaining civility is just too much of a challenge. At this stage in my life, I have absolutely no tolerance for abuse, and now this drunken dip-shit had crossed the line. I immediately pulled the cab over.

"Listen up, you, if it weren't for your infant child, I'd throw the whole lot of you out of my cab. But so help me if you don't mellow out, I will drag your nasty ass out of this cab and leave you."

He looked at me with pure hatred in his eyes. "I told you to shut your mouth." He punctuated his reply by poking my chest with two fingers.

"Keep your hands to yourself," I said, knocking away the offending digits. Now he took a swing at me, which I deflected with ease. This was a very big mistake. I reacted instantly popping him twice with my right fist. Both blows landed solidly, one on the nose, and one on the mouth. Now all Hell broke loose. The women were screaming, the baby was crying, and the men were shouting, one of them in Pakistani. The wife pleaded with me to take them home. She promised to keep her belligerent spouse under control. We weren't very far from our destination, and I did want to get the rest of this family home. Mr. Hostile Man was busy trying to stem the flow of blood from his nose, so we continued on our way. Within minutes we arrived. The women took the baby and idiot into the house, leaving the father-in-law to pay for the cab ride. Mr. Meter said $16. The man waited for everyone to go into the house, then he looked at me and burst into a wide grin. "I've been wanting to smack that arrogant bastard for years," he said, handing me two twenties. He told me to keep the $24 change, shook my hand, said this was the best ride he had ever had.

Chapter 22

I pulled up to the house at 48th and Folsom. It was a nice house in a nice, upper class, well-maintained neighborhood. There was a large picture window revealing a tastefully furnished room and two rather animated individuals. One of them, a young black woman spotted the cab, came out, and walked over to the back door of my car. She got in, but did not close the door.

"He's usually pretty nice, but tonight he's all drunk and started calling me a 'nigger bitch.' I don't take that from no one, especially a fat, ugly, old white man." She took a sip off of a highball she had brought with her from the house. It was obvious that she too had been drinking, but she had most everything under control. Everything, that is, except her anger.

"Well, it sounds like it's about time for you to be getting out of Dodge," I observed.

"You got that right, Sugar, but I ain't got no money, and I've got to get him to pay for the cab ride," she said, jerking her thumb at the picture window.

Speaking of jerks, the fat, ugly, old white man to whom she had referred was standing there in his boxer shorts and holey, stained string t-shirt. It was not a pretty sight, and to add insult to aesthetic injury, while sticking his tongue out at us he had jammed his thumbs into his enormous ears and was wagging his fingers in the air. This was the last straw for the little lady in the back seat.

"Oh yeah?" she said, getting out of the cab. "Oh yeah?" she said once again. Smiling and nodding her head, she took one last pull off of her drink, and just like a Big-League pitcher, she hurled it at her tormentor, right through the rather large picture window.

He had ducked just in time. The flying highball glass left behind an almost perfectly round hole in the window. All three of us stared, transfixed, as nothing happened for maybe five seconds, and then the remaining glass in that very large window shattered and fell like some crystalline waterfall. He stood there uncomprehendingly, with what was perhaps the dumbest expression I have ever seen on anyone's face. And trust me, I have seen some real dumb expressions.

She came back to the car and said, "Well, I guess I ain't gonna get him to pay for this cab ride."

"Hop in," I said, "You just got yourself a free ride home. And by the way, you just gave me another chapter for my book." I looked in the mirror as we pulled away, and it seemed as if her smile filled the back seat.

Chapter 23

I had arrived five minutes early for a 4:45 A.M. time call in Laguna, a new development in South Sac. It was so foggy that the porch light barely illuminated the front porch. I was wearing a black trench coat, along with black pants, Fedora, boots, and fingerless gloves. I wrapped on the door with my four-cell Mag light. A man in his late twenties opened the door, looked at me for a moment and then asked hopefully, "Are you the cab?"

"No, I'm not," I replied.

"You're not?!" he said with concern. I could see him trying to figure out why someone who looked like Guido, the Detroit hit man, was paying him a visit at such an ungodly hour.

"No," I said, in a deadpan voice, as I turned and shined my flashlight in the direction of the car. The beam from its halogen bulb burned through the fog. "That's the cab, I simply drive it."

Relief flooded his face, then he

started to laugh and said that was one of the funniest things anyone had ever said to him. I told him that I was often mistaken for a two ton, four-wheeled vehicle. This made him laugh even harder.

My attire inspired him and he donned his own black outfit, including trench coat and hat. We drove up to the airport looking like the Blues Brothers.

Chapter 24

I was dropping off an elderly gent with a cowboy hat and a western shirt at the Gas Log Lounge on Fulton. It was about 11:30 on a chilly Christmas Eve. Just prior to pulling into the parking lot in front of the bar, a tall black fellow tried to flag me down. As the old timer was slowly extracting himself from the cab, my next passenger approached.

When the front seat was finally vacant, I motioned him to get in. "I was just too cold to walk any further," he said. He appeared to be in his mid-30's. He gave me his destination and after I turned up the heat, I switched the radio from the country western music my previous passenger and I were enjoying to a jazz station. We tuned in just in time to hear a solo trumpet begin to play a haunting and wonderful rendition of "Silent Night."

We both were captivated and said not a word as we drove. Our hearts were pierced by that trumpet player putting his soul into playing that most simple of Christmas carols. The timing was perfect. We arrived at our destination just as the last trumpet note was fading. We were both deeply moved and had shared a special moment.

"This is a free cab ride. Merry Christmas, my friend," I said, extending my right hand to him. He grabbed my offered hand and clasped it to his heart.

"God bless you" was all he said as he swiftly left the cab. I have never been so graciously thanked.

Chapter 25

I was dispatched to see the man in room 2011 at the Sacramento Hilton. As I emerged from the elevator on the twentieth floor I heard muffled voices echoing down the hallway. Sure enough, room 2011 was the source of the disturbance.

"They look fine!" a male voice boomed. Although a female voice replied, I could not make out her answer. I mentally rolled up my sleeves and girded my loins before rapping on the door. A man in his fifties opened the door wearing an exasperated scowl. His face brightened when he saw me.

"Come in," he said. "I want you to look at something." I stepped into the room and he gestured towards a woman clad only in black panties. She was not unattractive and appeared to be in her mid-forties.

"Look at those," he said, continuing to point in her direction. "Aren't those some of the biggest, most beautiful tits you've ever seen??"

"They are quite impressive," I said diplomatically. In fact, they were huge. Quite out of proportion to her rather slim frame.

"This is not what I had in mind," she said quietly.

"There's just no pleasing you, is there?!" he bellowed. "I paid $4,000 for those. You'd think she'd be just a little grateful," he whined at me plaintively. I began to worry that this maniac might think up some kind of a taste test and decided to change the subject.

"Is there something I can do for you in the way of cab driving? You did call Yellow Cab, didn't you?" I asked, hoping that perhaps they had given me the wrong room number.

His face lit up. "Are you the cab?" he asked.

I noted a couple of empty quart bottles of whiskey and decided against my usual feeble attempt at humor.

"Yes," I said simply, not wanting to complicate this situation any further. He put an arm around my shoulder, gave me a $20 bill and asked me to get him a pack of smokes.

"Keep the change," he added. You might think that $20 was a lot to pay for a pack of cigarettes. I thought so too. Until the morning the computer sent me to pick up the lady whose car had broken down at the Highway Patrol Emergency Roadside Callbox Number 84-310 located 15 miles south of West Sacramento on Jefferson Boulevard.

I arrived shortly before 5:00 on that still dark and very cold April morning. There I found a woman patiently waiting, but no vehicle was in sight.

"Are you the lady with car trouble?" I asked, hoping I hadn't come all this way for nothing.

"I lied about the car," she admitted. "Otherwise the Highway Patrol wouldn't have sent me a cab." She climbed into the back seat. "I need a pack of cigarettes."

"And where do you suppose we'd find those this time of day?" I asked somewhat dubiously.

"The 7 Eleven in West Sac. And then

I need to come back here," she replied without hesitation.

"That's going to be quite a cab ride," I observed. The unasked question about her ability to pay hung in the air.

"This should cover it," she said, giving me three $20s.

"That it does," I said, heading north towards the 7 Eleven, where she purchased one pack of Marlboro Reds. By the time we returned, the meter read $63. I didn't bother with the extra 3 bucks. Every time I think I've seen it all.

Chapter 26

In case you're wondering who should get your vote for Village Idiot, I have the perfect candidate. I picked him up along with another newly released guest from Rio Consumnes Correctional Center, otherwise known as R-Triple-C. The Sheriff was paying for the ride back to the downtown jail located at Sixth and I. Most people I pick up at the South County facility are so grateful to be getting out that they are very nice to me. The fellow sitting up front with me fit in that category.

It soon became apparent that the guy in the back seat qualified for being one of history's monumental assholes. He had sense enough not to cross the out-and-out abuse line, which would have given me enough justification to pull over and throw his nasty ass out of my cab. Periodically he would belligerently ask if I knew what I was doing or where I was going. I pretty much shined him on.

While this occupation gives me the opportunity to occasionally kick a butt, which desperately deserves kicking, it is not something I am overly eager to do. I try to be very judicious with my application of violence. I do not feel compelled to prove my masculinity with brutality. That fundamental attitude, combined with the fact that I was nearing the end of my shift and simply did not have the time for a potentially messy situation prompted me to cut this obnoxious dipshit in the back seat a lot more slack than he would normally receive.

He maintained that he had been unjustly arrested. "After all, I only slapped a faggot, which couldn't be any worse than slapping a bitch," he whined. When I pointed out that "bitch-slapping" could get him busted as well, he seemed genuinely surprised.

Just prior to arriving downtown, the rocket scientist in the back seat announced that he needed a ride to Citrus Heights, insisting that I do it for $21, which was all the money he had. Mind you, he didn't ask me if I would take him -- he demanded. When I told him the fare would be at least $35-$40, he still demanded.

We pulled up in front of the jail. The fellow in the front seat thanked me and got out. The charmer in the back seat decided to give diplomacy one last try.

"So, you're not going to take me for the 21 bucks?" he snarled.

"No way, no how, now get out," I said, half hoping he would make a move. Sure enough, he didn't disappoint me. He had removed his personal effects from a large plastic Ziploc bag. As he removed himself from the back seat, he crumpled up the Ziploc bag and hurled it at me along with the epithets "Fuck you" and "asshole."

With that he took off running up the street. Glad to be rid of him, I brought the cab back to the yard and punched out.

While cleaning out my car, I found the Ziploc bag recently thrown at me. I noticed that it was not empty. When I flattened it out I discovered my pal's last $21. Yes sir, that was quite a parting shot.

Chapter 27

It was about 11:30 on a Saturday night. I was sitting in front of the Hyatt hoping to catch a fare from the big party going on inside. The festivities were breaking up and people were starting to leave. Most of them were elegantly dressed. I was standing outside the cab gossiping with some other drivers.

A drop-dead beautiful woman came out of the hotel entrance. She was wearing a tight-fitting shimmering black dress, which seemed to perfectly match her shimmering black hair. She was wearing large diamond earrings and was truly stunning. At her side was an impeccably attired black man. They both appeared in their late twenties. While I pride myself on maintaining my composure, even in the face of searing beauty, I found that, like my companions, I was unable to take my eyes off of her. The young gentleman, noticing the attention she was getting, naturally took it personally.

"It's all right, boys," he called out. "It's the nineties, we get to go out together nowadays." He pointed to himself and his partner.

Now it was my turn to take his presumptive accusation personally. I walked towards the couple standing by the late-model, very expensive European sedan. I adopted a pleasant expression to try to lesson my menacing demeanor. My 6'2", 240-pound leather-clad body made my attempt an exercise in futility. The fellow was slight in build, and although I could tell he was apprehensive, to his credit he adopted a defiant stance.

"I was simply appreciating a very attractive young lady," I said, gesturing to his companion. "Who she chooses to spend time with is none of my damned business. But let's set the record straight here, friend. I just look like a Ku Klux Klan motherfucker, I’m really not. I have fought hard for social justice all my adult life. Anyone riding in my cab gets treated the same way I would want to be treated, regardless of their race. I believe in the words 'Judge a person not by the color of his skin, but rather by the content of his character,' and I don't like being stereotyped any more than you do."

He smiled, "I was a bit hasty with my judgment."

"That's okay," I said smiling in return. " Here's my card. If you ever need a ride or you're too twisted to drive, call me. I'm a lot cheaper than the Sheriff. Strip search is optional in my car, and don't worry, bud, you're not my type." They both laughed. He thanked me for my card and for speaking with him. Before returning to my cab, I turned to the young lady, tipped my hat, and simply said, "Ma'am." I was rewarded with a warm, dazzling smile I will not soon forget.

Chapter 28

"Where are we headed?" I asked the still slightly sleepy lady as she settled into the back seat.

"Sutter Memorial," she answered.

"Are you a doctor?" I inquired.

"No, I'm a social worker. I help children and their families get through the 'hospital experience.' I explain the routines and procedures so that the child has a better idea of what's going to happen. After they're prepped for surgery I stay with them until they're anesthetized so that they're not alone."

"I hope you realize how important your work is," I said earnestly.

"Yes," she replied. "But sometimes it can be so very difficult. The children and their families I deal with are severely stressed and frightened, and sometimes the kids don't make it."

I proceeded to tell her about my "hospital experience." I was born with six perforations of the wall separating the lower chambers of my heart. I had open-heart surgery in 1963 when I was 15 years old. Mine was a particularly complicated procedure performed when this technology was brand new. Although the surgery itself was successful, I was soon besieged by a host of complications. My condition turned very sour. After a week, the situation had deteriorated to the point where my only hope for survival was a second open chest surgery. Even then the odds were slim.

To operate on me in my weakened condition was very risky, but to do nothing would inevitably and swiftly lead to my demise. I was prepped, transferred to a gurney, and taken up to the surgical floor. I was parked in the hallway while the operating room was being prepared for business and the surgical team was assembled. I spent the next 45 minutes strapped to that gurney all by myself. I realized how grave my situation was and that these could very well be the last conscious moments of my young life.

I was very frightened. People in surgical gowns were walking up and down the corridor ignoring me. I wanted desperately to reach out and grab someone's -- anyone's -- hand. I have never in my life, ever, felt so completely alone.

We were stopped at a traffic light. I turned and looked at her. She had tears in her eyes. "I know that your job can be terribly hard, but please, you must understand how very important your work is."

"I do now," she said, her eyes locked on mine. "When things get rough I'll remember your story. Thank you for sharing it with me."

The night before my surgery I wrote my first poem:

How can it ever be

That one day I will lie

For all eternity.

And that these eyes

Will never again be used to see.

Although others have died

Surely this could never happen to me.

Yes, in my youth, I was convinced

That I would never die.

And on this I look back with a sigh

From here in the Grave, where I lie.

I realize that this is not a particularly good poem but it does describe a 15-year-old boy, coming to terms with the reality of his mortality.

Chapter 29

I want

To lay with you and hold you in my arms

So that you can hear the beating of my heart

I want

To gently stroke your face, your hair

With magical fingers that make you tingle with contentment

I want you

To feel safe, warm and loved

I want you

To be more comfortable in my arms

Than anywhere you've ever been before

And I will whisper soft, sweet words into your ear

And I want

Those words to caress your heart,

Embrace your soul, and fill them with joy

"That was wonderful, Lou!" Sasha's bedroom eyes were even dreamier than usual. She exited the cab and seemed to float to the front door. Her young male companion, Alex, gave me a five-dollar bill to satisfy Mr. Meter and then slipped me an extra $10.

"Thanks for warming her up, Lou" he said with a lusty glint in his eye. He leaped from the cab and literally bounded to the front door. I like sharing poetry with my passengers. Most of them seem to enjoy it, and people often request my recitations. Sometimes my poetic offerings have unintended consequences...

She was in her mid-forties. I picked her up at the main entrance of Mercy General Hospital. She got into the back seat and gave me her destination. She declined the stick of Doublemint. I could tell she was upset, but she maintained her composure. After a while she asked if I had to work late.

"All night long," was my reply. "I've written a poem about it. Would you like to hear it?" She answered affirmatively.

All night long I roam these streets

Picking up drunks, sweethearts and freaks

Night after night I am in my car

Rushing to the hospital

Or sitting and waiting in front of some bar

Night after night I am in my car

Hauling around strangers

Can really get bizarre

Sometimes I'm bored, sometimes I'm scared

Sometimes I'm listening to a heart being bared

But all night long I roam these streets

Looking for those drunks,

Sweethearts and freaks

"That was great," she said. "It sums it all up, doesn't it?"

"Well, it's what I do."

"Have you written any other poetry?"

"Yeah, but the rest of my stuff is romantic." She hesitated a moment and then asked to hear another poem.

Come, my love, press your ear to my chest

Can you hear it?

Can you hear the beating of my heart?

This heart beats for you

From the very first moment our eyes met

This heart has beaten for you

And if I never, in my life,

Get to be with you again

The very last time that this heart beats

It will beat for you

When I finished, I heard her softly sobbing. She told me she had just that night lost her husband of 17 years to a heart attack. I felt terrible. Of all the poems to give her. I tried to apologize, but she told me that as difficult as it was to hear, she was glad I had shared it with her.

When we arrived at her house the meter read $13.40.

"This is a free ride," I said. "And please accept my condolences." She thanked me for the offer, but insisted that I take $20 and refused the change.

Chapter 30

Fast Eddie was a smoothie. I guessed him to be in his mid-Fifties. He was tall and trim always impeccably dressed and manicured. I never saw a strand of his silver-gray hair out of place until the night I picked him up at the Palomino Room as it was closing.

I had deposited him there five hours earlier, giving him plenty of time to get fully anesthetized, which is exactly what he did. Fast Eddie was an accomplished drinker. I could always tell that he had been drinking, but he had always remained in control. This night, however, he was sloppy, and had an edge of belligerence I had never before encountered when transporting him.

I opened the door. He crashed into the front seat. The suit coat he had always previously worn was crumpled in his lap. I noticed the initials SGN. They were stylishly embroidered on the cuff of his shirt. Perhaps Fast Eddie wasn't who he claimed to be. I strapped him in. For most of the short drive home he was slumped forward, muttering. He soon became agitated and in a plaintive voice kept asking how many more he had to kill. This ride sure got heavy quickly. We arrived at Fast Edie's apartment building and it was obvious that I would have to get him to and through his apartment door. I left him collapsed on his over-stuffed recliner.

A couple of nights later I picked Fast Eddie up at his apartment. He was waiting outside as usual and had returned to his same old fastidious self. I decided he needed to know what had happened. I asked him if he remembered leaving the Palomino Room the other night. I'm afraid that my bolt out of the blue question took him by surprise. After a while, he sighed, and admitted that the last thing he remembered was talking to a good looking redheaded lady at the bar, and the next thing he knew he was waking up on his recliner with a historically significant hangover. I told him that I was the one who left him semi-conscious on his La-Z-Boy. I told him about the muttering.

"Look", I said. "None of this is

any of my business but I think that you need to know what happened. If you indeed have a cover it may have been seriously compromised." He asked me to take him home. When we arrived back at his apartment he wanted to know if he had paid me for my services the other night.

"No," I said. "But that's okay. I knew you were good for it." He gave me a $50 bill and told me to keep the change.

That was the last time any of us ever heard from Fast Eddie.

Chapter 31

It was around 11:15 on a Wednesday p.m. So far, I was doing pretty well. I had just dropped off in Rancho Cordova and was trying to make it back downtown to the Amtrak station at 4th and 'I' in time for the 11:40 out of San Francisco. Suddenly a message flashed on my data terminal:

TRIP OFFERING ZONE 501

8400 FOLSOM BLVD.

I was right on top of the call, so I hit the "TRIP ACCEPT" button and received the complete trip information:

8400 FOLSOM BLVD.

College Green Light Rail

Station

For Chris

I popped off Highway 50 at Watt, turned right onto Folsom Boulevard, and was at the light rail station within 5 minutes. Two young black kids were waiting. As soon as they got into the cab I knew I was in trouble. They were both really nervous. Were obviously fiending. The vibes were very bad.

I knew they were up to no good. Without giving me a destination, one of the young men directed me to turn left here, go straight, turn right, another right, and now a left. We seemed to be going in circles. It became obvious that they were going to try to rob me.

I was finally directed to stop. We were at the corner of Premier and Huntsman. When I pulled over the meter read $6.60. I said they could make it $6 even "because I never sweat the small change, life is too short for that."

While saying that, I turned around and looked at the passenger in the right rear seat. He was just getting out of the car and was silently encouraging his friend. One look at his face was all I needed. I floored the accelerator and my cab took off. At that moment, the youngster still sitting behind me stuck a knife to my throat and screamed, "Give me your money!"

With the pedal still to the metal, making no attempt to steer, not even looking through the windshield, I jammed my right thumb between the blade and my jugular. My thumb was sliced open clear to the bone. My assailant proceeded to plunge the knife repeatedly into my chest. Luckily for me, each potentially lethal blow was stopped by one of my ribs, and although my chest was punctured and bruised, no serious damage was inflicted.

In fact, going for the chest was a big miscalculation because it gave me a chance to grab the knife. Had he stabbed me in the side of the neck or behind the ear, I would have been unable to defend myself and would have surely sustained grievous bodily damage. Indeed, I may not have survived at all. My leather gloves allowed me to get a good grip on the blade and actually take the knife away. By this time, we had picked up speed and had sideswiped a parked pick-up truck. We also sideswiped a fire hydrant and were now headed for a house. It was very noisy, which must have been nerve-wracking for my attacker, and may have contributed to his poor tactics.

Now I had the knife. Not knowing what other weapons my passenger might be carrying; I still believed that I was fighting for my life. I jabbed the knife backwards at the murderous little prick behind me just as my poor cab smashed into a house at high speed. The force of the collision threw the guy forward and I sensed that the knife had connected. To my satisfaction, there was a yelp of pain from the back seat.

The cab was halted by the house we had just hit. My passenger jumped out of the car and ran down the street. I shifted into reverse and, to my surprise, the cab backed away from the house. So, I gave chase.

I saw him turn the corner to the left. While keeping the running man in sight, I picked up my microphone and switched the radio from Data to the Voice channel. I yelled, "Mike I need you now!"

"Go ahead, Yellow 11," he immediately replied, using my radio designation.

"I have been attacked and have sustained numerous stab wounds...some of them to my chest and neck...I am by the corner of Premier and Huntsman. I have the assailant in sight."

I was lucky to be working with Mike. All of the dispatchers would have done their best to help me, but Mike had been a fireman (until being injured on the job) and had experience dealing with emergencies. More importantly from my standpoint, he had been a Yellow Cab driver for many years, and knew what it was like to be scared behind the wheel of a cab.

By the fourth word of my distress call, he was dialing 911. Simultaneously he sent a flash message to the data terminals of all in-service Yellow Cabs:

LOU SOLITSKE HAS BEEN ATTACKED AND STABBED

NEEDS IMMEDIATE ASSISTANCE

LAST REPORTED LOCATION WAS

HUNTSMAN AND PREMIER

The fellow I was chasing ducked between two houses. By the time I got there he was nowhere to be seen. I gave Mike the location. There was blood everywhere and my microphone was getting slippery and becoming increasingly more difficult to hold. I was getting light-headed and was concerned about losing consciousness. My lust for continued combat was starting to wane.

I returned to the house with which I had collided and encountered someone I assumed to be a resident. He was surveying the damage and was trying to come to grips with the destruction before him. He was still in his jammies and was holding a piece of my bumper. When I arrived, he held up the twisted piece of rubber and metal, looked at the smashed front end of my cab, and asked in a rather plaintive voice, "Is...is...this yours??"

"I'm afraid so," was my weary reply.

I heard distant sirens. Soon afterwards Sheriff cars, fire trucks, ambulances, and cabs started to arrive. A helicopter was circling overhead, illuminating the area with his searchlight. What had been a quiet neighborhood 15 minutes earlier had become very busy, noisy, and bright. All in all, it was quite a scene.

I was telling a deputy the last known location of my hapless assailant. He was radioing the information to other units in the area and the helicopter. Then I proceeded to tell him what happened. I became somewhat animated and the poor paramedic who was trying to render first aid said, "Hey, do you want to stop swinging your arms around? Look what you're doing to this guy's driveway." I looked down and saw that I was throwing blood all over the place. It was not a pretty sight.

I was taken to the Emergency Room at Kaiser North. While waiting to be seen I tried to figure out why I was still alive. I concluded there were two major factors contributing to my survival. First and foremost, my gloves, without which I never could have taken away the knife. Secondly the poor tactics employed by my would-be murderer. Going for my chest was a big mistake. Whatever the reasons, I'm confident that this was one cab ride my young adversaries would not soon forget.

The ER doc thoroughly checked me over. I had been stabbed or slashed seven times. My various wounds were cleaned, stitched where necessary, and dressed. A cab was dispatched to take me home. As much fun as my night had been so far, I knew that for me the worst part of the ordeal was yet to come. Telling my wife Jackie.

Chapter 32

The balding young man ran from the car rental terminal at the Sacramento Metropolitan Airport. I opened the front door and he jumped in.

"Where we headed?"

"The Dole rally, and pronto, please."

"No problem," I said, "But you'd better buckle up, partner."

Bob Dole was just wrapping up his unsuccessful bid for the presidency in 1996. There was a big rally in Old Sacramento.

"Are you with the campaign?" I asked.

"Just covering it."

"Which medium?"

"Print."

He worked for a national magazine published weekly. Ah, this should be a fun ride, politics being one of my passions. I've worked on numerous presidential and local campaigns since the '60's and here I was riding with a nationally published journalist.

"I believe we in this country have the very best government money can buy," I observed.

"You've got that right," he chuckled.

"Really," I continued. "As much as I hate to agree with Jerry Brown about anything, when he talks about money poisoning the system, I believe he's right on the mark. How much time and energy do you think our elected officials and their staffs are spending raising money for their next elections?"

"A lot more than they should be," he replied, nodding his head.

"And what's worse," I thundered on, "Once these people get into office, they're much more interested in taking care of their big-time contributors than they are concerned about taking care of their constituents. So, I'm reduced to having to vote for Clinton because I believe the people who have bought him off think more like I do than the people who have bought off Dole. Tell me I'm wrong!" I briefly took my eyes off the road to meet his.

"I can't. You're not," he agreed.

"Don't we deserve better?" I rotated the extended thumb of my clenched fist back and forth between the two of us.

"So, what's your solution?" he challenged.

"Glad you asked," I replied. "Strict campaign spending limitations."

"The Supreme Court has always shot them down as a violation of First Amendment, which guarantees freedom of speech."

"Sometimes rights conflict with each other. As Oliver Wendell Holmes said, 'The right to move your fist is limited by the proximity of my jaw.' I believe the right of the American people to have fair, honest, and effective officeholders far outweighs the rights of those seeking to buy politicians and elections!"

My passenger regarded me in silence for a moment. "Some of my most interesting conversations have been with cab drivers."

"This surprises you?" I asked.

"Nope, not at all."

We had arrived in Old Sacramento. I pulled up by the press buses parked on Front Street. As he was paying the fare I apologized for inflicting my political diatribe upon him.

"You've really given me something to think about," he said, shaking my hand before swiftly departing.

Chapter 33

"How long have you been driving?" she asked from the back seat. Normally I would have answered that I had been driving since 8 o'clock, but as we sped through this night our mission was grim.

The woman had received word that her 15-year-old son had been in an automobile accident. One of his legs was seriously injured. We needed to get to the Trauma Center ASAP. While still driving safely, our speed was greater than it normally would have been with a passenger on board.

"Since 1963." I answered.

"You drive this car like it's part of you," she observed appreciatively.

I love to drive. My father taught me when I was 15. Although I drive fast, I do not drive recklessly. My fast driving has earned me a few encounters with the law, although I've only received one ticket since 1974.

Early one morning I was exiting the Capitol City Freeway at El Camino.

This off-ramp has lots of tight turns, and although I never lost traction, I probably was going a wee bit faster than I should have. At least that's what the cop who pulled me over thought. As he approached my car, I could tell that he was not happy. The expression on the face that appeared at my window confirmed my original impression of anger -- this lad was hot.

As always, I had my California drivers' license, my cab license, the car's registration, proof of insurance, and a note from my mother ready. As I offered him this bundle of documentation, he looked at my face and recognized me, saying "Didn't you give that crazy, drunk old guy a free ride home so I wouldn't have to bust him on Christmas Eve about three years ago?"

"Guilty as charged," I replied.

"Alright," he said after a moment's thought. "I'm going to cut you loose this time, but you'd better slow the fuck down!" The last four words were delivered at the top of his lungs.

I snapped a smart salute and said, "Message received loud and clear, Officer. And gratefully."

Once again one of life's little axioms was reaffirmed: What goes around, indeed sometimes comes right back at you.

Chapter 34

He was young, black, and had a single stripe on the sleeve of his Air Force uniform. An aura of intelligence, intensity and clarity emanated from him.

"Headed home for the holidays?" I inquired.

"Yep."

"Where might that be?"

"New York City."

"Which borough?"

"The Bronx. South Bronx."

"Busy place," I observed.

"It can be challenging," he agreed.

The South Bronx has a major drug problem. The many cocaine smokers make it a very dangerous neck of the woods.

"We should legalize rock and give it away for free," I said.

"Yeah? Sounds like you're high on something right now to be thinking like that," he sneered at my suggestion.

"Nope. I'm sober as a judge. I feel a responsibility to be at least slightly less fucked up than the people I haul around."

He laughed in spite of himself. A good sense of humor also seemed to be a strong component of his personality.

"I have thought this out," I continued. "Every hand that has held a gun to my head, plunged a knife into my chest, hit me with a club, or tried to slit my throat has belonged to a young black man who looked like he had recently run out of rock cocaine, so I know what I'm talking about. Six times they have tried to rob me. They were successful only once. Those guys got the drop on me. I had an automatic stuck into my ribs and two pointed at my head. They got my cash -- Hell I would have written them a personal check. But in my fourteen years of driving cabs and six robbery attempts they were the only ones to get a penny from me."

"Sounds like you've been paying your dues out here," a modicum of respect creeping into his voice and his eyes.

"Yeah, well it sure beats working for a living," I replied. "Let's face it," I continued, "I'm not the victim of choice. I'm 6 foot 2 inches, and weigh 250 pounds. The little old grandma who just cashed her social security check is a much more desirable target. I see the victims out here all the time. I took a man to the E.R. with his upper and lower lips slashed completely open with a straight razor. If users got their drugs for free the people back home in your neighborhood would be a lot safer."

"If you think about it, it really is a rather draconian solution. Give a user an unlimited supply of rock and they fundamentally have to two choices: Leave it alone, or die. 'Cause once they start smoking, most of them won't stop until they're dead.

"I hate to sound hard-hearted, but as far as I'm concerned it would simply be a civic beautification project. I would provide programs to help people kick it. It would also be a powerful educational opportunity. We could video tape some of the more gnarly O.D. deaths and have youthful ex-users, not lame old cops or teachers, take them around to schools and show the kids the rampant paranoia, the seizures, them soiling themselves, and finally the death. The presenters could say something like 'You think drugs are fun? You think drugs are stylish and sexy? This is what they are really all about. There, but for the grace of God go I, and if you're smart, you would never get involved with drugs in the first place.'"

"That's pretty brutal," he observed.

"Yeah, it's strong medicine, all right," I agreed. "But we are trying to fight a deadly and widespread disease, and the tactics that have been employed thus far simply do not work."

We were passing the Marysville Boulevard off-ramp from I-80.

"If we get off here, I can get you to a rock house within 5 minutes."

"Yeah? Well what about all the people who go off and do violent and crazy things after smoking your rock?"

"Lock them up," I replied. "They're doing crazy and violent things now. Not only would those crimes decrease because there would be fewer smokers, but there also would be far greater police resources available to deal with these problems sincc the cops will no longer be chasing drug dealers or possessors. Nor would the cops have to deal with the crimes committed by people who no longer have to steal, rob, and kill to get drug money. The thousands of jail cells currently occupied by non-violent drug offenders could be made available for those criminals who hurt people, making this country a lot safer and saving a lot of money. Speaking of money, the economic impact on the inner-city areas would be profound. A lot of the money spent purchasing drugs comes from people living the poorest neighborhoods and most of that money goes right out of the country. In a safer environment, all that money could be spent at the legitimate businesses which would surely return, generating revenue and jobs, as well as providing goods and services not seen in these neighborhoods for years."

"You really have thought this out," he grudgingly observed.

"You bet I have. I am threatened with the potential of drug-generated violence every night. It is a reality of my daily existence, and I have seen the misery and suffering it has caused."

At that moment, we were arriving at the United Airlines terminal at the airport. I retrieved the young airman's bags from the trunk.

He paid the cab fare and then said, "I have never, ever, ever tipped a cab driver." He reached into his wallet and produced another dollar. His eyes locked on mine. He slowly extended the bill towards me.

"Here, man, you've earned it."

It was not the largest tip I have ever received, but it was certainly one of the more meaningful.

Chapter 35

She was in her late fifties and came from somewhere in Nebraska. I picked her up at the Amtrak Station. She asked me to take her to the Jibboom Street Bridge. When we arrived, she told me to pull over and wait. She got out of the cab and stood by the rail for a long time. I was beginning to wish that I had asked for my money up front in case she decided to jump.

After a while she came back to the car. She had been crying. She pulled a small camera out of a carry-on bag and took several photographs of the spot on the bridge at which she had just been standing, and of the adjacent roadway, then asked to be taken to the Vagabond Inn across the street from the train station. She explained that ten years ago, that night, her 23-year-old son had been killed by a teenaged girl, high on methamphetamine, at that very spot. She needed to go there and say a prayer for her dead boy. For more than a decade this woman had suffered because of the thoughtless actions of some fool who thought it was OK to drive while under the influence of that terrible drug.

◆

I was on my way to the Zebra Club to pick up a regular customer named Scooter. I've hauled him around for years and have become quite fond of the good-natured, big-hearted lad. Scooter's gregarious personality has made him very popular and many of his friends have also become my regular customers. Scooter will not let his friends drive drunk, and has covered many a cab ride home for his inebriated pals. Helping to keep these young people alive and out of jail has become part of my mission out here.

As I pulled up in front of the club I encountered Nick. He was climbing onto one of those super-sleek, super-fast Japanese motorcycles. The kind that looks like it's doing 80 while it's standing still. Nick was one of the friends I met through Scooter. His face lit up when he saw me. He reached out to shake my hand and nearly lost his balance. It was clear he had been drinking a lot.

"Hey, Nick, why don't you let me take you home?"

Thanks, Lou, but I'm fine."

"No, you're not! You're all fucked up. Let me get you home, free ride. Come on, be a pal."

"Lou, really. I'm okay."

I looked around and tried to find Scooter, who would be a big help in this situation. At that moment, Nick took off. The bike flew down the street leaving behind the high-pitched whine of its heavily revved engine. In an instant the taillights became a fading memory.

The police report estimated that Nick was traveling in excess of 100 M.P.H. when he broadsided the parked pick-up. He was thrown over the truck and smashed headfirst into a garage door. Within 10 minutes some friends who had planned to meet Nick at his home found him. Although he was not yet dead, Nick never regained consciousness, and he died before reaching the hospital.

◆

The mother and her three kids were waiting for me as I pulled up to the curb in front of the U.C.D. Sacramento Med Center. They were not a pretty sight. Half of the woman's head had been shaved so that a long gash on her scalp could be sutured.

One of the little tykes had his arm in a sling and had lost all of his front teeth. A little girl had a cast on her lower left leg and was walking with crutches. An even smaller child had his tiny neck in a brace. After gently helping them into the car and securing them with seatbelts, we headed for their home.

On the way to a movie they had been broadsided at high speed by a drunken driver who had blown a red light. If the drunk driver were merely jeopardizing his own life, limb and property, that's one thing, but innocent people often must bear the consequences of someone else's irresponsible and thoughtless actions. I wish I could visit this moronic Cretin in his jail cell so I could properly repay him for what he had done to this unfortunate family.

◆

Speaking of moronic Cretins, I had pulled up in front of the River Park Pizza Parlor. A man barely able to walk staggered out of the front door. As he lurched to his vehicle he waved me off saying something about not needing a ride. I walked over to his car. Through the rolled-up driver's window I could see him repeatedly try without much success to find the ignition with his key. I opened his door and said, "You'd better give me those keys, partner."

"Who are you?" he asked with all of the belligerence he could muster.

"Who am I?" I asked, with a pleasant smile on my face. "I'm the guy who's going to beat the shit out of you if you try to drive right now," I said, still smiling.

As he glared at me I reached in and grabbed the keys out of his fumbling hands. I went inside the pizza parlor and found the barkeep. I gave him the car keys, saying that the guy outside didn't want me to drive him home, but that he was in no condition to drive himself.

The bartender said that it was not his problem, and suggested I mind my own business. I could tell that he, too, had been drinking. I leaned over the bar and put my face close to his. I jerked my right thumb towards the car parked outside his door.

"I'm giving that vehicle's license plate number, along with the name of your establishment to my dispatcher, who will give that information to the Highway Patrol. If that car is involved in an accident, you, sir, will have a king-sized problem."

For a moment, I thought he was coming over the bar, which would have been just fine with me. I don't know if it was my size, dress, demeanor, or the look in my eyes, but something made him reconsider and the moment passed. Not surprisingly, I have never received a call from that pizza parlor again.

◆

The worst non-violent ride of my cab-driving career was rushing a distraught woman to the Sutter Memorial Hospital so she could be with her 18-year-old son before he died. He had been hit by a drunk driver, and I subsequently learned had not survived.

◆

I was asked to speak at Nick's memorial service. I spoke of the zeal with which he had lived his life, and how he had stomped on the Terra Firma. After speaking about how much Nick would be missed I concluded with the first two verses of Longfellow's "Psalm of Life."

Tell me not in mournful numbers

That life is but an empty dream

For the soul is dead that slumbers

And all is not as it seems

Life is real, life is earnest

And the grave is not its goal

Dust thou art to dust returnest

Was not spoken of the soul.

Chapter 36

I've had some pretty interesting encounters with law enforcement-types. Early one morning while we were still being radio-dispatched, I was headed east on Highway 50. I had been told to call the dispatcher for my exact information when I reached the 12000 block of Folsom Boulevard. As I approached the Hazel Boulevard off-ramp I contacted the dispatcher, who told me to pick up my passenger at the Sheraton Hotel.

Great! I should have gotten off the freeway at Sunrise Boulevard, the previous exit, nearly three miles back! Had I been given the correct information I would already have my passenger in the car. That is, if my passenger was still there. I had been running on the call for at least 20 minutes. I figured I had about a fifty-fifty chance of finding someone still there. My chances were diminishing with the passage of every minute.

I became enraged. How hard would it have been to get the correct information to me? I guess I wasn't deemed worthy of the effort! I had visions of my passenger getting into another cab and going all the way to Seattle! I screamed into the microphone clenched in my fist, "Why can't you get it right?!"

I didn't key the microphone on, but I needed to vent. I learned a long time ago that yelling at a dispatcher is like pissing into the wind, the results are invariably bad. So, the unengaged microphone ended up taking the brunt of my verbal abuse.

I am afraid my lane control may have slipped a wee bit during my tantrum. I have learned to control myself when I am in traffic, but heck, at 3 o'clock on a Wednesday morning; you pretty much have the freeway to yourself. There was only one other car on the road with me, and it was quite a way back.

Suddenly it came flying at me at high speed and -- yep lit up its red and blue lights. This morning just kept getting better and better. I immediately pulled over. A highway patrolman appeared at my window.

"Man, you were all over the road. What the Hell's wrong with you?"

I still held the microphone tightly in my fist and up to my mouth, slightly shaking. Slowly I turned my head towards him. My eyes were smoldering in a low gravelly voice I hissed through clenched teeth, "This dispatcher is making me crazy."

His eyes narrowed. Although he did not draw his weapon, he did rest his hand on it. "What do you mean?" he asked, cocking his head slightly to the left.

"I was sent to the 12000 block of Folsom Boulevard, which sounds like Folsom and Hazel to me," I replied.

"It is," he agreed.

"Well, when I arrived here, I checked in with my dispatcher, and was told to pick up at the Sheraton!" I said, becoming more animated.

"But that's back at Sunrise," he said, pointing down the freeway.

"You know that, I know that, and for as many years as this idiot's been dispatching, *he* should know that too!

Right now, back at the Sheraton a drop-dead beautiful woman probably is getting into some slob's cab and is going all the way to San Francisco! They're most likely going to be engaged by the time they get there!"

He laughed. I knew I had him. I delivered the coup de grace.

"If you give me a ticket, so help me God, I'll go down to your personnel office, get an employment application, and give it to our dispatcher. I'm sure you people pay a lot more than we do. And then you can work with this guy!"

"That's okay," he said. "We've already got some real winners working for us. I understand exactly how you feel. Just be a little more careful in the future."

My passenger, miraculously still there, was actually waiting for me at the Shell Station at 13000 Folsom Boulevard.

Chapter 37

We had been waiting in the parking lot of a scummy apartment building in Rancho Cordova for nearly 20 minutes. The man sitting in the right front seat had become increasingly agitated.

"Damn!" he finally said. "I hope she's coming back."

I had picked up my passenger along with a very attractive young lady at the Pine Cove Bottle Shop. He wanted to go to the Motel 6 in Rancho Cordova. She said we had to make a stop in Oak Park along the way. It was obvious these two were not going to choir practice. We pulled in front of a rock house. The lady hopped out and from the reception she received it was clear that she was a regular customer. We proceeded to the motel in Rancho. While the man was paying for the room, the young angel of the night suggested that we "ditch this dildo, go smoke up the rocks ourselves, and have a real good time."

I told her that I just look like a chump, but even I'm not stupid enough to connect up with and trust a coke-smoking hooker from hell. The same, however, could not be said of the man with whom I was waiting for this sweet young thing to return.

"You don't have anything to worry about," I said with confidence. "After all, you have the drugs."

"No I don't," he said. "I gave her all $120 worth at the motel, plus an extra $50 for her company."

It all became crystal clear. Back at the motel she said that her girlfriend had a real nice pipe they could use as long as she got a couple of blasts. So, here I sat waiting with this rocket scientist, who had not only given this working gal all of the drugs, but $50 as well.

"I hate to be the bearer of bad tidings," I said. "But she's not coming back."

"She's not, is she."

"Hell, no," I said. "She already tried to get me to help her ditch you!"

"Why didn't you say anything to me?" he demanded.

"Because I didn't think you were stupid enough to give her all of the drugs!" was my less than diplomatic reply.

A flicker of anger flashed in his eyes, which was replaced with resignation. He had indeed been had. No, this one wasn't going to win any awards for deep thinking. We returned to the motel where surprisingly, they refunded his money and then he had me drive him back to Sac.

Sometime later I picked up a lady named Connie at the Safeway on Alhambra. Connie was no other than that coke-smoking hooker from hell who had performed the famous disappearing lady act in Rancho Cordova four months earlier. She didn't appear to recognize me. She asked to be taken to Rancho Cordova with yet another stop in Oak Park on the way. When we reached Rancho, we went to the same scummy apartment complex.

"I have to go up to my apartment to get your money and a big tip. I'll be right back," she said nodding and smiling. My God, I thought, she must think all men are idiots. But I played along.

"All right, I'll be waiting right here," I said innocently. She got out of my cab and swiftly disappeared around the corner. I slipped out of the car, whipped off my hat, and peeked around the same corner in time to see her enter an upstairs apartment. I climbed the stairs and rapped heavily on the door with my four-cell Mag light.

"Who is it?" a man's voice boomed from behind the still closed door.

"I'm looking for Connie," I replied. Now the door flew open. There stood one of the ugliest sights ever inflicted upon these old eyes. He was at least 6 foot 5 inches tall and must have weighed over 300 mostly flabby pounds. What little hair he had left was flame red. He was clad only in his all-too-brief BVD's.

"What do you want with my wife?" he bellowed menacingly.

"All I want from your wife is the $32 she ran up on my meter. I am Yellow Cab," I said, not backing of an inch. This guy was obviously used to throwing his considerable weight around.

"I'm not giving you a fucking penny," he said, glowering at me.

"No problem," I said, with a very pleasant smile. "I'll have the dispatcher call the Sheriff, and I'll have him suggest that they bring the dogs. So, you'd best be getting rid of the drugs that Connie brought home with her."

"What!?" he screamed, his ruddy complexion now became crimson. For a moment I thought he was going to make a move, which would have been just fine with me. Instead, he snarled, "Can you change a hundred?"

"No problem," I said, smiling once again, which only added to his fury. He left the door and returned shortly with a $100 bill. I peeled off his $68 change. As I turned to leave I asked him to thank Connie for calling Yellow, and smiled yet again. I have never heard a door slammed so enthusiastically.

Chapter 38

Although I didn't know this particular piece of violin music that was playing on the classical music station, the style was familiar. I couldn't decide if it was Schubert or Mozart. I was parked in front of the Hilton waiting for a 5:45 A.M. time call. My passenger appeared. She was a young woman in her mid to late 20's, smartly dressed, more appealing than attractive. I took the bags she was carrying and she gracefully slid into the back seat. With the luggage safely in the trunk, I climbed in and turned around to ask for her destination. Her eyes were clear and bright. They met mine directly as she said, "To the airport, please."

Her smile was captivating. This woman had an aura of composure and calmness that bordered on serenity. The dawn was breaking over the high Sierras on the eastern horizon and the sky was ablaze with brilliant shades of reds and blues. A particularly beautiful passage of violin music was playing softly on the radio. Everything was right -- the music, the dawn, and the company combined perfectly to form a magical environment.

Somehow, I knew that my passenger could tell me whether we were listening to Schubert or Mozart. I asked her if she knew who composed this piece of music.

"Why, yes," she said, somewhat taken aback. "I was trained as a concert violinist. This is Schubert, although, you are right, it is very reminiscent of Mozart's style."

I asked if she was in town to perform.

"Goodness, no," she said, and explained that she was currently in the Air Force. I asked where she was stationed. "South Dakota," she replied.

"You're in missiles?"

"Yes."

"Do you turn keys?" was my next question.

Her answer was another soft "Yes."

Her voice was lovely, my brain was

numb. This saint-like apparition in the early morning light was employed by the U.S. Air Force to command a flight of intercontinental ballistic missiles.

Whoa! I joke about being attracted to heavily armed women, but sitting behind me now was one of history's monumentally armed women. If she received the proper orders, her job was to initiate a sequence of events that would culminate with the incineration of millions of mostly innocent people, many of them children. They would be the lucky ones. More millions would be horribly maimed, with a good portion of them to die slow, agonizing, deaths. People would suffer as a result of this woman's actions for generations.

What has happened to our humanity that allows us to train a rare, lovely soul such as this to do such inhuman things to so many people? My mind was genuinely boggled. We discussed nuclear defense policy. I voiced my opposition to the MX missile and extolled the virtues of the doctrine of Mutually Assured Destruction. She said that my overall grasp of nuclear strategy was so sound that I should be teaching at the National War College.

In what seemed like no time at all, we reached the airport. She tipped me generously. As I handed her the bags, I asked her if she knew where her birds were targeted. She said yes. It makes a difference whether you're taking out the ICBM complex at Lapuda or the city of Kiev, which has hundreds of thousands of kids.

Next I did something terrible. I asked her if she could do it. Her clear, bright, direct eyes widened slightly in amazement that I could ask her such a question.

"Do you mean if I receive the codes?" she asked in reply.

I nodded. She stepped closer, keeping my eyes fixed. She almost imperceptibly shook her head as she quietly said, "I don't know."

After an eternal moment, she broke eye contact and that wonderful woman who had been trained to kill millions, gracefully glided into the terminal.

Chapter 39

I had dropped off in West Sacramento and was headed back to town. I was turning left onto West Capitol Boulevard from 5th Street, when a 1970s vintage four-door Cadillac pulled up in the right turn lane. There were six men riding in the car. They were all looking at me like I was a 16-ounce Porterhouse steak and were talking among themselves. I turned left, looked in my mirror, and was not surprised to see them behind me.

I floored the accelerator and soon was going more than 50 in a 25 M.P.H. zone. I looked in the rearview mirror again and sure enough, the Cadillac was still right behind me. No doubt about it, I was being chased. I blew the stop sign at 3rd and West Capitol, and made a screeching right-hand turn. I pulled into the left lane as I approached South River Road, signaled a left turn, and at the last moment, broke right -- tires screaming once again.

Now I floored it and soon had the speedometer pegged at 85 m.p.h. The

Cadillac was gaining on me. The four-cylinder engine of my Chevy Lumina was no match for the Caddy's big V-8. It was obvious that I had no hope of outrunning this malevolent monster. My pursuers pulled along my left side. The front passenger window lowered and the man sitting there pointed a large black automatic pistol at me. He was holding it sideways, which is always a bad sign.

"Pull over, mother-fucker!" he shouted at me.

I was on the varsity judo team at San Jose State for four years. I was taught to use my opponent's size, weight, and momentum against him. I slammed on my brakes, catching the other driver by surprise. Although they were faster, my lighter car with its advanced technology brakes was able to decelerate a lot more quickly than they could. The Caddy shot past me. The arm with the gun tracked back, but events were occurring too rapidly and the gunman didn't have time to take a shot.

When I had lost enough speed, I cranked the wheel to the left and made a high speed, four-wheeled drifting U-turn. The Cadillac was at least a quarter mile down the road with its driver struggling to turn it around. I scurried down South River Road and turned right onto the Tower Bridge crossing the Sacramento River. About halfway across the river I glanced into my mirror and saw the Cadillac turning onto the bridge. I slid to the right onto Front Street, then immediately executed a vicious left, tires squealing, onto Neesham Circle leading to Old Sacramento. Realizing that I would soon be amongst lots of people, including many cops, my would-be robber friends broke off their pursuit and continued down Front Street at high speed.

As I mentally prepared myself to complete the rest of my shift, I silently thanked the judo coach, my "sensei," who so long ago gave me the training, which helped me to escape this band of desperados.

Chapter 40

I was trolling for fares at the Holiday Inn. No one wanted a ride so I decided to head up J Street. As I was leaving the Hotel's parking lot, a man flagged me down. I opened the front passenger door and he tumbled into the seat.

He looked at me while trying to focus his eyes, and inquired as to his whereabouts.

"We're in Sacramento," I replied.

"Oh," was his pained reply. "I want to go to Oakland."

"That will cost you a hundred dollars," I said.

"Okay, but I need to get to an ATM."

Great! So far it had been a horrible night, but this one ride would turn everything around. We went up to the San Wah Bank on the corner of 8th and J. I watched him stagger up to the cash machine. He couldn't get his card into the slot. I walked over to the ATM, took the card (which he was holding upside down), and put it into the slot. I requested instructions in English. The machine asked for the PIN number.

"The ATM wants your PIN number," I said, pointing to the number pad. He started to punch in numbers so I turned around, not wanting to see his code.

Tap...tap...tap...tap...Beep...

Tap...tap...tap...tap...Beep...

Obviously, my twisted new friend was having trouble remembering his PIN number. This amusing little routine was broken when, after his fifth unsuccessful attempt, the machine took his card and told him to contact his bank. He looked at me with his bleary eyes and said, "I have over $3,000 in that account."

Great. Four little numbers. How many undamaged synaptic pathways do you need to remember four little numbers? Four numbers. That's all that stood between me and a $100 trip to Oakland, which would have been the salvation of my night. Four little, single-digit, positive integers!

My would-be long distance passenger looked at me. "What do I do now?" he asked bewilderedly. I realized that as bad as my night was, I wouldn't want to trade places with him. After all, he had made a genuine effort to get the money.

"How much cash do you have on you?" I asked. He emptied all of his pockets and came up with a grand total of $8.53. I called Greyhound, and was told that a ticket to Oakland costs $12. I took him to the bus station at 7th and L. Mercifully there wasn't a line at the ticket counter. We walked up to the agent and I gave my forlorn new buddy the additional four dollars he needed for a ticket home.

The bus to Oakland would depart shortly, so I made sure he was on it before I returned to my cab, where the computer informed me that I had just missed a trip to the airport. Proving, once again, that no good deed goes unpunished. Yes sir, this night just kept getting better and better.

Chapter 41

"Oh oh, this could be trouble," I said to myself, as I watched the excited doorman at Melarkie's jump up and down while waving his arms over his head. His antics had started the moment he spotted me entering his parking lot. This was an ominous portent. A doorman this happy to see me usually meant trouble. And trouble it was.

Just as I reached the entrance to the bar, the door flew open and out came five -- count them -- *five* -- glamorous beauties, most of them in tiny little skirts. They were shrieking and laughing as they descended upon my cab. Two sat up front with me, while the rest piled into the back. The lady next to me grabbed my right knee with her left hand. The sweet young thing on her right was running her fingers through the rather longish hair sticking out from under the back of my hat.

One of them asked my name. I told them it was Lou. As we were headed towards our destination in South

Natomas, they were all singing "Louie Louie." Somebody lit up a joint and started passing it around. It was like a flashback to the '60's: Sex, drugs, and rock-and-roll. They told me their husbands were all away on a hunting trip. They were whispering and giggling amongst themselves. As we turned onto the street where one of them lived, a couple of them yelled, "Fuck!"

"What's wrong?" I inquired innocently. They pointed to two pick-up trucks with campers. One of them said, "Our husbands are home."

The one playing with my hair said, "Too bad. We had plans for you, Big Boy." If they indeed had such plans, and had the husbands not been home, I still wouldn't have participated for a number of reasons, most importantly the fact that I have been gratefully married for more than two decades.

But let's say that the husbands weren't home yet. And let's say that I did go into the house with those wanton women. Let's say the husbands came home…oh, about an hour later and found us in an embarrassing situation. These guys were just returning from a hunting trip. They'd all be heavily armed, and most likely drunk. I'd have exactly two chances of surviving such an encounter: Slim and None.

Just imagine being killed by five jealous husbands. I'd be a legend. I am convinced that it's better to be gone, but not forgotten than the other way around.

Chapter 42

I was picking up Scooter at Andiamo's, an Italian restaurant on Folsom Boulevard. They were having a big costume party for Halloween. When I arrived, Bobby, the bartender, walked over. He was wearing black boots, black pants, a black shirt, a black vest, a black hat, and black gloves. With great delight, he asked me if I wanted a cab ride. Later I found out that one of my regular customers thought he was dressing up like Zorro; however, all of his friends decided that he looked more like me, so he went along with it.

I must admit I was somewhat flattered. But it did give me cause to think: Here I am, a 50-year-old man, and people were dressing up like me for Halloween

Chapter 43

It was about 4 a.m. I was going up J Street towards the Hyatt at 12th and L. If there weren't too many cabs on the scene already, I would roost there for a while and surf the zones on my computer hoping to catch a call. Every once in a while, someone actually comes out of the hotel looking for a ride to the airport.

While waiting for the traffic signal at 10th and J, I noticed a man standing in the shadow of the doorway. He was looking at my cab and after a short while, nodded at me. He approached the car. I opened the front door; he leaned over and peered furtively inside. After a moment's hesitation, he looked up and down the street and swiftly jumped in.

"Where are we going?" I inquired.

"Just drive up J Street for a while."

"That won't work," I replied. "I need to know our destination." This was a volatile time of the morning. Knowing where this ride was going would help me plan my strategy.

"All right," he acquiesced. "Take me to Fair Oaks and Watt."

As we headed towards that intersection, my passenger was nervously looking around. He was checking out the interior of my cab. His nervous eyes lighted on my computer. He now peered at me more intently. I could tell he did not like what he saw.

"Have you ever heard of Operation Phoenix?" he asked suspiciously.

"Do you mean in Viet Nam, in the early '70's, when we teamed up with the local intelligence/thugs and eliminated all known Viet Cong, Viet Cong sympathizers, and anyone else against whom these clowns might have had a vendetta?"

In reply, he threw a $5 bill at me to cover the $3.40 fare, opened the door, and jumped from the cab. The problem was that we were traveling at about 15 mph at the time. He expertly rolled twice, landed on his feet, and ran into a convenient alleyway, thus disappearing. Oddly enough, he was not the only passenger ever to leap from my rolling cab...

I had picked up Daryl and his mother in a very low-rent district in Citrus Heights. Our destination and the fact that this was a round-trip made it obvious that we were on safari up the Zambezi, looking for the giant rock monster. It was equally obvious that Daryl and mom had been doing way too much already. Mom was handling it somewhat better, but Daryl was seriously blowing it. He was in no condition to be out in public. My guess is that he didn't trust mom to come back with the goods. So, he came along to keep everything on the up and up.

The problem was that fear was eating his brain. I'm sure that sitting up front with a guy who looked like a big, ugly, old, leather-clad, racist/redneck hit man was not doing anything to bolster his sense of security. His eyes bulged wide every time they lit upon me. I could almost see the gray matter dribbling out of his ears. The rampant fear that filled my cab became a tangible entity. Mom picked up on the inescapable vibes.

"You just settle down now, Daryl. You'd best not get us thrown out of this cab!" Daryl was now really freaking out. We were turning left off of Sunrise Boulevard. He grabbed the door handle, opened the door, and leapt from the cab. He tried to run, but he fell face forward and slid for a while. The whole time, his eyes were wide with terror. Soon he was on his feet again, and in a flash, he was gone.

I hit the brakes.

"What are you doing?" the woman screamed from the back seat.

"Stopping for Daryl," I said.

"Fuck Daryl!" was her vehement reply. "How much is on the meter?"

Just in case you were wondering who to vote for as Mother of the Year.... Damn, every time I think I've seen it all!

Chapter 44

"Where are we headed, Gents?" I asked the two falling-down drunk lads I had picked up at the Raven Club on J Street.

"To Old Land Park," said the one who was still able to talk. "But first take us by the drive-through at the Taco Bell on Folsom Boulevard." It came as no surprise that there were a lot of cars waiting at Taco Bell since it was one of the few fast food venues still open at this late hour. Ten minutes later, we were about halfway through the line when nature began calling one of my passengers. Actually, it was more like a scream.

"I've got to pee!" announced the fellow sitting behind me. I soon heard his door open. Holding onto the opened door with one hand to steady himself, he unzipped his pants, removed his plumbing, and in front of God and everyone in line, let fly. Many businesses that stay open all night employ off-duty law enforcement personnel as protection against robbery.

While my passenger was happily relieving himself a female deputy sheriff ran up to my cab.

"Why are you letting him do that?" she screamed at me while pointing at him.

"Hey, you're the one getting paid the big bucks to enforce the law, not me!" I bellowed back. "Unless he's pissing in or on my cab, I don't really care! He's just giving me another chapter for my book."

By the time we finished our heated verbal exchange, my now fully relieved passenger was climbing back into the cab oblivious to the drama unfolding around him. Although she looked like she wanted to shoot me, this frustrated deputy was now faced with a fait accompli and there was really nothing she could do to me.

"You better not let me catch you when I'm on duty," she snarled menacingly.

"I'll be looking forward to it," was my less than genuine reply.

Chapter 45

It was about 12:30 on a Saturday morning. I was trolling for fares. Driving slowly around places where crowds of people gathered, hoping to hear the magic word, "Taxi." I pulled up in front of the entrance to Charlie Brown's, a restaurant with a club in it called The Twist & Shout Lounge. Just as I stopped by the entrance, the large doors burst open and two security guards along with two bouncers came running out literally carrying what appeared to be a very drunken man. Once they cleared the door they all gave a mighty heave and sent the man flying through the air, Superman style. He landed in the beam of my headlights with his back towards me. He struggled to his feet and, as it did not look like he was going to fall again, I stayed behind the wheel. The man brushed himself off. When he turned around and saw my cab, he raised the index finger on his right hand above his head. With a leering smile and a glint in his eyes, he called, "Oh taxi!"

Oh God, I thought, what have you in

store for me this time? I like what Voltaire said about God. He claimed that God was a comedian playing to an audience that was afraid to laugh. I believe God truly is a comedian, and I have learned to appreciate her sense of humor. I had a feeling I was in store for another comedic episode. I opened the front door and the flying rowdy flopped into the seat.

"Get me out of here!" It was more like he was pleading than demanding.

"Would you care to give me a clue as to where you would like to go?" I inquired.

"Anywhere!" he replied.

"Well, we could be in Lake Tahoe by 3 a.m." I observed, just trying to be helpful.

"Great!" he said. "Let's go!"

"Really?" I asked, since Lake Tahoe was about $150 East of Sacramento. I wanted to make sure.

"Hell, yes!" was his adamant reply. Money appeared to be no problem for my newfound friend. It can be fun when you run into someone with more money than brains. It was winter and a small weather front had moved through Sacramento. It had produced very little precipitation in the valley, but I was concerned about road conditions over the Sierras. I recalled the weather report predicting a "light dusting of snow" at the higher elevations. Just to make sure, I called the 24-hour CalTrans Road Information Service. It said that all highways were open and clear. I decided to go for it.

By the time we hit Placerville we were in a blizzard. We came to a CalTrans checkpoint. The man inspected my tires and decided to let me through. Shortly afterwards I heard on the road condition channel on the radio that chain restrictions were applied to all vehicular traffic. At the time, I was driving Yellow 11, a fully depreciated 1986 Ford LTD. The defroster stopped working at low temperatures, and soon a layer of ice had formed on my windshield. After a while I could only see through a silver dollar sized hole in the ice directly above the defroster vent.

I really should have turned back, but by the time we returned to Sac, I would have invested more than two hours of my time for nothing. I couldn't very well charge my passenger for a Tahoe trip if we never made it to Tahoe, so I was highly motivated to continue heading east.

By this time the road was covered with ice. I had to slow to 25 mph. When driving on ice it is important to keep your speed and direction slow and steady. Any sudden changes could cause the car to lose traction and slide out of control. This kind of driving takes a great deal of concentration. The challenge of my situation was compounded by the fact that I had to keep my face smashed against my windshield so I could see through the tiny hole in the ice pack that had formed on the glass surface.

It was at this moment that my still drunk companion decided to confide in me the fact that he had been abducted by aliens. He claimed that the creatures that had snatched him had come from a different part of the galaxy. He said that the CIA had been chasing him and probably had us under surveillance at that moment. He informed me that they were after him because he knew "The Truth". He knew that every American president since the Kennedy administration had in fact been an alien.

This conversation was doing nothing to contribute to my ability to concentrate on the road, but I persevered. After what seemed to be an eternity we finally arrived at the South Shore of Lake Tahoe. Our harrowing experience seemed to have brought us closer together as human beings. I believe that some sort of bonding must have taken place because by the time we reached the lake everything my demented passenger had to say made perfectly good sense to me.

Chapter 46

Long trips are one of the serendipitous joys of cab driving. I get a lot of long trips. Part of this I chalk up to the regular deposits I make at the Karma Bank. More than anything else I have ever done; this occupation offers me situations where I can make a difference. All one has to do is be up front with me.

I ran into a young lady by the Med Center one very cold, late winter night. She had two small children dressed in heavy little coats with hoods, which were cone-shaped. The thoroughly miserable woman also had two large bags of groceries dangerously perched on the stroller in which she carried her pointy-headed little tykes.

I put the stroller and groceries into the trunk of the cab. The lady strapped her two youngsters and herself into seatbelts. She told me her destination. Inwardly I shuddered for her and her small children. Hers was a very dangerous neighborhood, a gruesome manifestation of helplessness, hopelessness and lack of dreams, goals or aspirations. This is the brutal environment of an ever-increasing segment of our population, which is becoming incapable of pulling its own weight. People who don't believe they have any future at all.

This type of environment spawned that 11-year-old monster who shot and killed a little girl in order to gain entrance into a Chicago gang. He, himself, had been treated at area emergency rooms for numerous cigarette burns inflicted by his 15-year-old, crack smoking, prostitute mother.

It was just such a neighborhood into which we were headed. It breaks my heart to think about that little lady, surely no more than 16 years of age, trying so hard to be a good mother, yet having to raise her little ones in such a dangerous place.

As we pulled away from the curb my passenger told me to let her out when the meter reached $7 since that was all she had.

"You keep your $7. You get home for free." We both knew this was at least a $15 ride. If a person is in need and is up front with me, they usually get home for however much money is in their pockets. Sometimes the ride ends up being free. One of the things I do is get stranded people home, regardless of their ability to pay. All they have to do is let me know what's going on from the very beginning of the ride, and not treat me like a chump.

Well maybe I couldn't do anything about where this little mother lived, but I sure as hell could - and would - get this family safely home.

"God bless you," she smiled, as she sighed. "You must be a Christian."

"No, but I really like the part about loving and caring for one another."

"Well you sound like one to me, and you certainly act like one."

I took this as a compliment. My next ride went from Apple Computers in Laguna all the way up to Yuba City for $135.

Chapter 47

It was 6:10 a.m. I informed the dispatcher that I was clear on Freeport Boulevard. She told me to call for my complete information when I reached the 3200 block of Riverside Drive. As I arrived at that block a man started to wave furiously when he saw me. He was in his early forties, stuffed into a powder blue 3-piece suit, which was at least two sizes too small. With wild eyes, he tried to open my back door. I opened the front door for him.

"I want to sit in the back," he shouted.

"You can't," I replied. "I don't ride single males in the back seat. I'd be happy to call another cab for you."

"Hey, I have to catch a 6:50 flight!" he almost screamed.

It was now 6:19.

"Well," I said, and motioned to the front seat. With great annoyance, he climbed into the cab.

He pulled out a cell phone and said, "I'm going to report you to your dispatcher."

"The number is 444-2222," I said, helpfully.

He glared at me. When he reached the dispatcher, he told her his name and said he was a doctor.

"Your driver would not let me sit in the back seat and has been very rude to me!" he complained. Then he gave his office phone number and demanded that the owner of the company call him, and with that, he hung up.

Trying to be helpful once again, I spelled the owner's name for him.

"Don't be a smart ass," he snarled. "Just shut up and drive."

Oh, yes, this guy was a real charmer. Normally I would have immediately thrown his nasty ass right out of the cab, but since he was stressed from being so late for his flight, I decided to cut my amusing new friend a little bit of slack.

I pulled over, took off my sunglasses, and looked him directly in the eyes.

"You now have two choices," I explained evenly. "You can let me give you your best shot at catching this flight, or you can continue to behave like an arrogant prick, but you don't get to do both. Your choice."

He turned bright red. It looked like his head was going to explode. A vein was pulsating on his left temple, and for a moment I thought he was going to stroke out, which would have thrown me into overtime. He realized that I had him by the short & curlies.

Finally, voice quivering, he said, "Take me to the airport." And with almost a superhuman effort, he added the word "please."

"Alright," I said, nodding. "You'd better buckle up, doc. We've got some traveling to do."

As he put on his seatbelt, I hopped onto Business 80 at the 15th Street onramp. The morning was beautiful. A particularly soothing piece of piano music was softly playing on the radio. I swiftly, but safely wove my way through the moderate traffic, and 15 minutes later we exited I-5 at the airport.

It would still be close, but he would probably make his flight. As we were driving towards the terminal I explained how I had been slugged in back of the head one night, which is why I wanted single males to sit up front. He said he understood.

We arrived at the terminal. The now calm man paid the fare, gave me a very generous tip, and thanked me for the excellent cab ride.

Chapter 48

I was delivering a bottle of Sutter Home white zinfandel and a pack of smokes to Candy, a very attractive, young paralegal, and the mother of three little girls. She is semi-divorced and resides in a nice suburban neighborhood. I've hauled Candy around for years and late at night if she doesn't feel like driving she calls me for deliveries.

While she was paying me, my phone rang.

"Hey, Lou. This is Artie and Hal from New York City! You picked us up earlier. Do you remember us?"

"Yeah, I dropped you guys off at the Double Tree. What can I do for you?" I queried.

Artie's voice became audibly softer, and conspiratorial. "Hey, man, we were wondering if you could hook us up with some honeys."

"You mean professionals?" I asked.

"Yeah, man, you seem hip. I'm sure you've got connections."

As a matter of fact, I do occasionally transport beautiful ladies who seem to stay busy all night and, while I do know a couple of young lovelies who would be glad to accommodate these lads, I have too much to lose, so I play it straight out here.

"I just look like a pimp. I'm really not," I replied.

"Hey, we're not fooling around here," Artie persisted in his New York style. "We'll pay $500 to any broad you send over here, and we'll take care of you too," he added unnecessarily.

"Five *hundred* dollars?" I repeated with raised eyebrows. Candy's eyes lit up. She pointed to herself and mouthed the words 'I'll do it.'

Well, that was a bolt out of the blue. You could have knocked me over with a feather! I regained my composure enough to give Artie the number of a "full service" cab driver. After I hit the "end" button on my phone I looked at her incredulously and said, "YOU'LL DO IT??"

She placed a hand on either side of

my face and then moved hers closer to mine. Looking directly into my eyes and smiling an alluring smile she said, "Darling, I worked my way through college 'DOING IT!'"

Damn!

Chapter 49

Every time I think this book is done I meet a new knucklehead. There is a theory that maintains that we men have enough blood for our brains or our dicks, but not both simultaneously. Whoever formulated this theory must have known the piece of work currently being transported in my cab.

He had floated out of the bar. I opened the front door and as soon as he toppled in he started to describe the most beautiful woman he had ever seen. This woman was a goddess. She had it all. She was smart, she was funny. She smelled great. All in all, she was the loveliest lady upon whom he had ever laid his eyes. This guy was carrying on like a high school kid. An immature one at that! And he had to have been in his late fifties.

I was beginning to suspect that most of my new buddy's blood supply was residing somewhere south of his cranial region at the moment. My suspicions were about to be confirmed. With stars in his eyes he continued.

"She smelled so great she lit up the

whole place when she made her entrance. She came and sat right next to me! I got her phone number! I gave her mine!"

Suddenly he slapped his hands to his face. His mouth dropped open. His eyes bulged wide. "Oh my God!" he screamed.

"What's wrong?" I asked.

"I'm married," he replied. "To a judge," he added softly.

I whistled. "Well, you certainly weren't wearing your thinking cap tonight, were you?"

"I sure wasn't."

My guess is he will be hovering around the phone for the foreseeable future trying to head off disaster. Yeah, every time I think I've seen it all.

Chapter 50

I picked her up in Greenhaven at around 11 p.m. She sat up front. The pheromones were flowing. This could be interesting and dangerous I said to myself. But like the moth to the flame I let the scene play out.

She was not beautiful or endowed with a gravity defying body, but she was profoundly appealing. We were headed to a warehouse in a light industrial park across town. She was a history major at Sac State. We clicked tongue-in-groove intellectually and I enjoyed her quick wit. All too soon we arrived at the warehouse. She paid the fare along with a ridiculously large tip, which she insisted I keep. She said that she'd need a return ride in three hours and asked if I would mind coming back at 2:30 a.m. for her.

"Wild horses couldn't keep me away," was my reply.

A young man opened a door, stuck his head out and when he saw the young lady he smiled. He took both of her hands and they beamed at each other.

Illuminated by my headlights it was like a scene out of a Ron Howard movie.

Two hours and fifty-five minutes later I was waiting at the door. Five minutes after that she appeared. My lights were off and I swear she seemed to glow in the dark. She floated towards my cab, a serene smile on her face. I was witnessing an apparition and the whole scene had an unworldly quality about it. Once again, she sat up front.

"Home?" I asked. She simply nodded.

We rode in silence for a couple of miles and I was content to bask in the radiance of her aura. Whatever happened in the warehouse had touched her deeply? After a while she slowly turned her gaze upon me. I started to tingle.

"May I share something with you?" she asked tentatively. I felt comfortable with this woman and intuitively knew she was worthy of my trust.

"Sure," I replied, trying not to sound too eager.

"Okay," she said. "I want you to repeat after me, *Nam...Yoho...Ranga...Kyo"*

I repeated the phrase and within a short period of time was able to say it perfectly. We started to chant. At first, we repeated the phrase...

Nam...Yoho...Ranga...Kyo. Over and over again with a fairly mono-tonal intonation, but then it subtly began to change.

Nam...Yoho...Ranga...Kyo...

Nam...Yoho...Ranga...Kyo...

We chanted over and over again as we drove through that magical night.

Nam...Yoho...Ranga...Kyo...

Nam...Yoho...Ranga...Kyo...

Over and over again. We seemed to melt into one another. Then our molecules and atoms were spread across the horizon for as far as the eye could see. We became one with each other and the two of us became one with the entire universe.

Nam...Yoho...Ranga...Kyo...

Nam...Yoho...Ranga...Kyo...

Over and over again. She led, I followed. I led, she followed. We both followed. Before we knew it, we were in her driveway with our eyes locked.

Nam...Yoho...Ranga...Kyo...

Nam...Yoho...Ranga...Kyo...

Over and over again. Her eyes were on fire. Her nostrils were flaring.

Nam...Yoho...Ranga...Kyo...

Nam...Yoho...Ranga...Kyo...

Over and over again until we reached a crescendo and she had to stifle a scream. Then she reached out and hugged me. No kissing, just that wonderful hug. She sobbed softly. After a while she pulled away, looked at me in the eyes, touched two fingers to her lips and then gently brushed them against my lips. Then she left.

I made sure she got into the house safely and as I drove off into the morning I'm sure I was leaving a trail of stardust and moonbeams. I never saw her again.

Chapter 51

It was about 3:30 a.m. The computer

told me to pick up Chuck at a very nice house off of American River Drive. The man was waiting on the front porch. He came limping towards the cab as I drove up. His clothes were disheveled and torn. I opened the front door and he collapsed into the front seat. He looked back at the house and then slowly turned his gaze towards me. In his haunted eyes, I could see a mixture of fear and almost terminal satisfaction. His mouth was dry and with some effort he was finally able to exclaim, "They were sisters…and chiropractors!"

It took some time after that for the young man to remember where he lived.

Chapter 52

The call was at the Vagabond Inn at 3rd and J. I was instructed to see the clerk. When I walked through the door the man behind the desk recognized me and informed a guest talking on the phone, that his cab had arrived.

He was a thin man of medium height. He had curly brown hair and a silly little moustache. With great annoyance, he hung up the phone, turned to me and said, "No! No! No!" in a very irritating voice. "In Switzerland, the cab driver does not arrive until the passenger is ready!" he exclaimed patronizingly.

Oh yeah, I like this guy already. Normally I would have walked back to the cab, locked all the doors and driven away, but the Vagabond was a very good customer and the desk clerk was a pal. So, I decided to let my new foreign friend into the cab.

I opened the door from inside the car. He got in and asked, "How much to go to Mercy General Hospital?"

"Between $6 and $7 depending on the lights," was my reply.

"You will do it for $5," he commanded. I really enjoy being ordered about by supercilious, prissy little bastards like this guy, and normally respond very well to this type of approach.

I fixed his eyes with a not particularly friendly gaze and said slowly, "If $5 is all you're giving me, when that meter reaches $5 you're outta here.

"That's all I'm giving you," he said, handing me some folded $1 bills, which I stuck into my pocket. As we headed up J Street I decided to give my new Swiss buddy some unsolicited - but well deserved - advice.

"If you want a cab driver to cut you some slack, treat him with civility and respect. Don't come on like some arrogant asshole." He didn't say anything, but sat there and fumed until the meter flashed $5. I immediately pulled over. We were at 30th and J, ten blocks from the hospital.

"Here's where you get out," I said

pleasantly.

"I demand that you call the police and the Swiss Consulate. You have insulted Switzerland!" he screamed, barely containing his rage.

"Just get out!" I said, with no little annoyance. I reached over and opened his door. He began slapping me with open palms on my right arm and shoulder. He had crossed the line and physically struck me, but I never felt threatened or justified in hitting him back, although he did desperately deserve to get his ass kicked.

A police car drove by and I decided to get them involved before things escalated. I honked the horn and waved at them, catching their attention. When they pulled over my passenger leapt from the cab and ran towards the policemen.

"I must get to Mercy Hospital!" he cried.

"Hey, we'll take you to the hospital," one of the young cops said, looking at me as if I were some kind of greedy cretin.

"NO!" was the emphatic reply. "I

demand that you arrest this man!" he screamed, pointing at me.

"Why? What did he do to you?" asked the officer, looking at him with concern and at me with malice.

"He was rude to me and he insulted Switzerland!" was the somewhat crazed reply of my former passenger. I just smiled.

"What's this all about?" the other cop asked, pulling me aside. I told him that I had picked up the guy at 3rd and J and he had demanded that I give him a $6 or $7 cab ride for $5.

"All he had to do was ask. Hell, if it were an emergency I would have taken him for free. Instead, he ordered me to take him for the $5 as if I had no choice." The cop nodded. My explanation obviously made sense. The Swiss charmer now was working himself into a lather.

"I demand you arrest this man!" he screamed again, saliva splattering from his mouth. The police, who had no intention of arresting me, now became the object of his wrath. "If you don't arrest him I'll…I'll…Break out the windows of your police car."

Well that will certainly show them, I thought. Boy, this guy really knew how to make friends.

It was nearing the end of my shift and the cops were now much more interested in him than they were in me. I asked if I could leave and one of the officers said I could. I climbed into my cab. As I drove off I could see the Swiss fellow gesturing wildly in my rearview mirror as both cops were pulling out their nightsticks. Welcome to America, I thought.

I pulled out the small wad of ones he had given me. Ironically, I counted $6, which would have easily covered the fare to the hospital.

Chapter 53

I was parked in front of the Double Tree Hotel waiting for a UPS Air Cargo crew scheduled for 20:15 pick-up. I like hauling around UPS pilots. I figure in most cases they are somewhat less likely to try to rob me, although I have been warned that if I have a cab full of management captains I should keep my hand on my wallet at all times.

While waiting, I leaned against my cab and played my harmonica. After a while a lady walked over to me and in a heavy French accent asked if I was a romantic person.

"Hopelessly," I replied. She nodded, smiled and said, "Aaahh."

"Would you like to hear a romantic poem?" I asked.

"Please."

I am usually driving while inflicting my poetry on the captive audiences in my car, which necessitates keeping my eyes on the road. This time, however, I was free to lock up my unsuspecting victim's eyes with my own.

I drink you in with my eyes

You refresh my thirsty soul like an oasis in a parched desert.

You fill my ears with the music of your intellect, poetry, laughter and wit

Even though our hearts will never beat together as one

I love the times when yours is beating not so very far away

No matter how far the distance between our two beating hearts may grow

I will always cherish the memories of the times we've shared

And as long as this heart of mine continues to beat

The magic of those memories will never fade

My eyes never once left hers. As I recited we became connected. My gaze bore ever more deeply into her soul. I could see and feel her react to the words that were flowing from my mouth through her ears into her heart. We two strangers stood there alone, oblivious to the activities swirling around us. Suddenly for one brief moment we were the only two people in the entire universe.

She became unsteady and had to reach out for support on the nearby stair railing.

"Are you okay?" I asked softly.

Saying nothing she nodded affirmatively. She stood away from the handrail. Impulsively she gave me a big hug and without another word hurried into the hotel. It was then that I noticed the three grinning UPS pilots standing at the top of the stairs.

"Up to your old tricks, I see," Captain Tiegs said as I was putting his leather flight bag into the trunk.

"It's a tough job," I said, "But somebody has to do it."

◆

I drive the crew to Mather Field in Rancho Cordova. We arrive at around 20:40. I retrieve their luggage from the trunk, open the gate for them and as they walk by wheeling their bags behind them I give a smart salute while wishing them uneventful flying. I point out that it is better to be bored than scared. They all smile and one of them salutes in return.

Around 03:00 the next morning I get a call from Donanda at UPS Air Ops-Sacramento. She tells me that Captain Tiegs' 727 will be landing at around 03:40. I head out to Mather Field and park along the fence where I get a good shot at the runway. I scan the eastern horizon where an aircraft's navigation lights are barely visible. I get out of the cab to stretch my legs and get a better shot of the approach.

Sometimes I play my harmonica. The rabbits on the other side of the fence occasionally stop their grazing and hop over to investigate the strange sound. Sometimes seven or eight of them will congregate. They stand on their haunches, noses twitching, ears trained in my direction. I enjoy playing to this furry audience.

One morning I heard the far-off honking of geese. I searched the sky and, sure enough, there was a huge V-shaped formation of Canadian snow geese flying almost directly overhead. The light from the nearly full moon was dancing off of their flapping wings. It was a truly beautiful sight.

The approaching aircraft has turned on its landing lights and within a minute or two it is on the ground. As soon as the 727 touches down Captain Tiegs engages the thrust-reversers and throttles his three Rolls Royce TAY051-54 engines up to full power. Not only slowing the plane, but also creating an incredibly loud rumble that is felt as well as heard.

I watch the big plane taxi to its spot on the ramp. I back the cab up to the gate and pop the trunk. It's a cold morning so I keep the engine running with the heat on. I have a tape of soothing music cued up on the cassette deck. I get out of the cab, open the trunk and whip out my harmonica. Before long three brown trench coat-clad figures round the corner trailing their wheeled bags. I can tell by their walk that they're tired.

"Uneventful night?" I ask as I load up their bags.

"Yeah, just long," the flight engineer Doug Selby replies.

I knew what he meant, as I had been working since 16:00 the previous afternoon.

We all climb into the cab and I take this crew of tired old freight dogs back to their hotel.

Waiting by The Gate

The hour is late and I'm waiting by the gate

For those UPS pilots, who fly the freight.

Over the eastern horizon, I see a dim light

She's right on time, it's the Louisville flight!

I watch the approach, the landing smooth as glass

And hear those thrust reversers engage with a blast.

The gateway team is awaiting

A plane full of boxes

They are anticipating.

As that big 7 5 taxies, by

That tired aircrew heaves a grateful sigh,

Because they can see

My Yellow Cab parked by the gate

Waiting for them, those UPS pilots

Who have hauled all that freight.

Chapter 54

The computer had sent me to the Med Center ER for Sid, who is blind. As I pulled up in front I spotted a little old guy with a white cane. He turned towards the sound of the cab. This looked promising.

I got out of the car and asked him if his name was Sid. "Yeah," he replied. "Are you my cabbie?"

"You bet I am." I offered an elbow. He latched on and I guided him to the car. I buckled him into the front seat. He had a swollen blackening eye, a fat lip and numerous other bruises and contusions on his face.

"Jesus, don't tell me you got jumped."

"Nah, I was in a bar brawl," he explained. "But I won," he added proudly.

"What happened?" I asked.

"I had been drinking for a couple hours when this guy comes up to me and says that I'm sitting on his stool. I told him that I didn't see his name written anywhere on it. He told me that it didn't look like I could see much of anything. And with that, the guy grabbed a hold of my shoulder and tried to pull me off the stool! I reached over and grabbed his wrist and yanked his hand off my shoulder, hanging onto his wrist so I knew where he was, and started beating on his face. He got in a few good licks, but I kept hitting him and finally he went down for the count."

What a scrapper! I guess this bully picked on the wrong little old blind guy.

Chapter 55

It was 3:30 on a Sunday a.m. My cell phone rang.

"This is Lou," I answered.

"Big Lou," the voice on the other end replied. I recognized it immediately.

"Hey, Craig. What can I do for you, bud?"

"Lou, I need some evaporated milk and an eyedropper. I found a brand new little kitten. It's still wet!"

"All right, give me about 20 minutes," I said.

I went to the Lucky's at 56th and Folsom, which stayed open 24 hours. When I arrived at Craig's he had the kitten wrapped in a towel. It was so weak it couldn't even hold up its head.

Craig filled the eyedropper and I gently pried its mouth open. He then slowly released milk into its mouth. The kitten drank the nourishing liquid. It was so tiny and weak I was sure it wouldn't survive.

I didn't see Craig again for another week. I was prepared to receive the bad news, but against all odds that frail little new life persevered. Craig, God love him, stayed awake all night and fed the tiny critter every hour.

Within a couple of days, the kitten was doing better. Craig already had a cat that was not about to put up with a new roommate. So, he gave the kitten to a friend who could take it to work with her and keep up with the feeding schedule. Now the cat is healthy, happy and loved.

Chapter 56

I walked thru the door at the bar in the Red Lion Inn at the stroke of 2:00 AM. The lady barkeep and the bar maid both looked very relieved to see me. My two, soon to be passengers, were sitting at the bar.

"Your cab is here". The bartender announced.

"Are you the cab?" one of the patrons asked.

"No, I just drive it, the cab's out in front" I replied.

"What are you, some kind of wise ass?" he shot back with an edge of alcohol-enhanced belligerence.

"Every chance I get. I just can't pass up the opportunity" I answered honestly. Another feeble attempt at humor hits its mark.

The guy now starts to laugh. He sticks his hand out.

"I'm Phil, this is my brother Kenny".

I could tell Kenny was not completely comfortable with my appearance. Back then, I wore a black trench coat along with my black hat, pants, and gloves. Many people, including Kenny, thought I was some kind of undercover agent. I never could figure this out. Why, if I wanted to work under cover, would I dress up like Dick Tracy?

We climbed into the cab, Phil sat up front, and Kenny took the back seat.

"Take us to the nearest bar". Phil requested.

"It's after 2:00, the bars are closed." I informed him.

"Then take us to the nearest liquor store" Phil persisted undaunted."

"It's after 2:00." I said once again. "No alcohol can be sold in California."

Phil was beginning to get the picture. "Well, where can we get a drink?" he nearly whined.

"The closest cocktail to here is in Reno" I replied.

"OK, let's go there!"

"That's going to be expensive," I pointed out.

"Well, then you'd better run this for $500.00" he said handing me his AMEX gold card. "Is that going to get us to Reno and back?" he asked unnecessarily.

"You bet it is" I replied in a heartbeat.

Suddenly I saw Phil in a whole new light. As drunk as he was, he was easy to get along with. His brother Kenny was another story. He reminded me of Ratso Rizzo from Midnight Cowboy; a scrawny, sneaky, little speed freak with a high screeching voice. He leaned forward, so he was screaming nearly directly into my right ear.

"Why are you doing this to us. We don't sell drugs! We don't do drugs, we're not criminals. Why are you investigating us!?"

Louder and louder he screeched. He continued this abusive chant the entire 20 minutes it took us to drive to Roseville. Reluctantly, I realized that he wasn't going to stop. $500 dollars wasn't enough. There was no way in hell that I was going to suffer this for another 2 hours. I looked over at Phil and said

"So help me God Phil, if he doesn't shut the fuck up, I'm gonna smack him."

Phil nodded "Lie down Kenny. Shut up and go to sleep!" he commanded.

"Oh, OK Phil" Kenny shut up, lay down, and promptly went to sleep.

The rest of the trip was relatively uneventful.

◆

It was 2:15, on a busy Saturday A.M. I was returning from Elk Grove, where I had just deposited Inga and Rachel, a couple of Danish honeys. It had been a great trip and so far, the entire night had been going splendidly. A call had been holding on Marion Court in Old Land Park for quite some time. I accepted the call and asked Mike to confirm that the customer still wanted the cab. A few minutes later Mike informed me via the computer, that my prospective passenger was still waiting. I arrived just after 2:30 A.M.; a man was sitting on the porch. He staggered toward the cab. I opened the front door for him, and he toppled in. "I need a drink" he declared in a low, gravelly voice.

"It's after 2:00 the bars are closed." I answered"

"I need a drink." He rasped again, slightly louder.

" It's too late, no alcohol in California after 2:00 AM."

"I NEEEED a DRINK!" he repeated with increased urgency.

"Look" I said, in an effort to cut this unpromising conversation short, "The closest drink to here is in Tahoe."

" How much will that cost?"

"I'll get you up and back for $200.00."

He began to closely examine a disorganized wad of bills clutched in his right fist. He discovered, and retrieved, two crumpled $100 dollar bills.

"Will this get me to Tahoe and back?" He asked.

"You bet" I said, slowly shaking my head. People never cease to amaze me.

"Do you think we could maybe stay up there and gamble for a while?" his dull red eyes brightened. I figured the gambling bit was just a face saving gesture. Maybe he didn't want to admit to himself that his need for alcohol was motivating him enough to spend $200 and 4 hours in a cab with a total stranger simply to get another drink.

"I wait for 2 hours. If you want to stay longer, it will cost you $25.00 for each additional hour."

He came as close as he could, to thinking about it and decided that 2 hours should be enough time. He closed the door, and said "OK, let's go."

The reason he was holding the money in his hand, was because the boxer shorts and holey T-shirt he was wearing, didn't have any pockets. I suggested that since we were going to a Nevada casino, he might consider putting on some more clothes. He looked down, surveying his attire, then blurrily looked at me, and asked "Do you really think so?"

"Without a doubt."

He staggered back into his house. After a short while, he reappeared wearing some farmer's overalls and a pair of sandals.

Yup, my new buddy was really ready to step out and do the town, or maybe I should say the lake.

We arrived at Lake Tahoe at about 4:30 AM. I drove to the 7-11 at Zephyr Cove. My passenger stumbled in, and purchased a 12 pack of beer. He gave me the 12 dollars change and climbed back into the cab. I drove back into California, where I knew it was legal to drink in a cab. Within 10 minutes, he had downed 4 cans. A short time later, after he opted not to do any gambling, we were driving around Emerald Bay heading back to Sacramento. It was within 15 minutes of sunup.

The sky was crystal clear, and the scenery was breath taking. My passenger was having an alcohol enhanced religious experience, and I was his guru. As we drove along the west shore of the lake, the sun rose over a cloudless horizon. It blazed a shimmering, golden path across the surface of the water. What an incredible sight.

The rest of the trip back to Sac was downhill literally, and figuratively. My passenger proceeded to polish off the rest of the 12 pack. By the time we returned to his Land Park house he was unconscious. I woke him, and told him he was home. He gave me a $20 tip. He opened the door, took about 5 steps, and collapsed head first into some bushes. I shoveled his empty beer cans onto his lawn and turned the cab around.

I thought he was out cold, but as I was driving away, he waved feebly from his bush. $232 dollars for a 12 pack of beer! If I ever need a drink that bad, please just shoot me.

Chapter 57

Sean Higgins was one of my first regular customers. He hung out at Chargins, a neighborhood bar located at 49th and J frequented by aging jocks and colorful locals. Sean definitely fell into the latter category. He was a minor celebrity because he starred in the first local TV show spotlighting fugitives wanted by the Sacramento Police Department. He retired from the force as a lieutenant.

I stopped by the bar to pick Sean up just before closing time. He had yet to finish his drink. I didn't have anything pending so I hung out. He was holding court, explaining to some of the remaining patrons how he would handle various confrontations. In one situation, he would employ a choke hold while another time he would use his nightstick. He turned his gaze in my direction and after a moment of consideration he said "You, I just shoot you, you big son of a bitch." We all had a good laugh at that one. I miss Sean. He passed away in the early nineties and Chargins nor Sacramento has been the same without him.

Chapter 58

I knew it was a long shot that I would find anyone who still needed a ride when I pulled up in front of the Limelight at 2:20 A.M. What little chance there was seemed to evaporate as Ben from CO-OP Cab Company pulled up behind me and headed purposefully for the front door.

"Hey Lou." he said.

"Morning Ben."

I noticed a young man approaching our cabs. He was tall and thin with short blonde hair and many tattoos. I opened the front door.

"Will $20 get me home to G Parkway and Franklin?"

"Yeah" I replied. "Even if the meter says it's more, $20 will get you home."

It was obvious to me that something had devastated him.

He was in a state of profound emotional anxiety.

"Do you want to talk about it?" I

asked, as we headed south on Highway 99.

"My best friend killed himself tonight. Just as I walked through his front door he blew his brains out."

"Are you sure he's dead? Head wounds can be messy but they are not always fatal."

"Yeah." He said. "The cops came, and the paramedics said he was gone."

"What a waste." I observed.

"He was an alcoholic. I guess it all got to be just too much for him. I've had three close friends take themselves out in the last two years."

"I have found that death is a lot harder on the survivors." I offered. "Somehow that seems to be a comforting thought at times like this."

"Yeah, well I'm going to go home and listen to The Doors."

"Not 'The End' I hope." I looked at him with concern.

He actually smiled and feebly chuckled. "No, 'Break on Through to The Other Side.'"

I had a hunch about what he might be thinking. I put an Eva Cassidy tape into the stereo. It was cued to her version of 'It's A Wonderful World.' I cranked it up and the song finished just as we pulled up in front of his house. He looked at me with tears in his eyes. "It is a wonderful world, isn't it?"

"It sure is. Don't be in too big of a hurry to leave it, son. Suicide is a permanent solution to temporary problems. Here is my card. Call me if you ever need to talk." I extended my hand. "Lou's the name."

He shook my hand. "Thanks." was all he said.

Chapter 59

I pulled up to the Amtrak station shortly after 1:00 AM. She was tall and her long thin dress caressed her slender body like a summer breeze. As soon as I stopped she approached the cab and asked if I was available.

"I sure am. Hop in."

She sat in the back. "This train is going to be three hours late. Please take me to get a bottle of wine."

"No problem." On the way to the Pine Cove Bottle Shop, I dazzled her with my poetry and wit, if not my modesty. As we were returning to the train station she asked how much it would cost to take a cab to Chico.

"The Yellow Cab flat rate to Chico is $140."

"OK" She said. "Let's go!"

"I can't."

"Why on earth not?"

"I have three UPS air crews I have to transport starting around 3:45 this morning. There's no way I could ever make it to Chico and back in time."

"OK." She persevered undeterred. "Let's make it $200."

"Hey, the money's not the problem. I would love to take you for the $140. But I have no one to cover my crews this morning. I must be there for them and I can't do that if I'm taking you to Chico this morning. Einstein will not let me be two places simultaneously. He is very strict that way!"

My impassioned, almost whining explanation, impressed her not. Obviously, she was not used to hearing the word no. "What if I told you I'm not wearing any underwear."

"What?" I said looking back at her.

She spread her legs to prove her point, and prove it she did, beyond a shadow of a doubt. It was a sight I will not soon forget. She was bald and beautiful.

"I can't." I whimpered.

"What's the matter? You don't like women?"

"Come on. Give me a break. I love women. If there was any way I could, believe me I would. But I have people depending on me, and I will not betray their trust, not even for someone as beautiful and wonderful as you."

This woman clearly understood the "power of the pussy," that mysterious and irresistible force that compels strong and otherwise intelligent men to do stupid things. She wielded it like a weapon. She was the irresistible force, meeting the immoveable object but she finally accepted the inevitable. When we arrived back at the station, she gave me a $50 bill for the $12 fare, no change necessary.

"Pity." She said. "I'm sure it would have been a fun ride."

No doubt about it, I thought.

When I arrived home later that morning, I told my wife Jackie about this little adventure. She was really pissed off.

She said, "We could have used that 200 dollars!"

Chapter 60

When you first start driving a cab, you're known as a rookie, or a "FNG" - fucking new guy. A lot of people come and go in the cab business. Most of them don't stick around long enough to make any friends, and the old timers tend to be standoffish.

About three weeks into my cab-driving career, the dispatcher, Ron Parker, asked for drivers to back up Danny Cooper. A passenger had run out on Danny without paying the fare. I arrived about three minutes later. He looked at me. "You're that new guy, aren't you?"

"Yep. Lou's the name."

"Danny." He said, extending his hand.

"What's up Danny?"

"This asshole ran out on me, he's in Apartment number 3. Let's go."

" Ahhh...Shouldn't we wait for some other drivers?" I asked.

"Nope. Between you and Betsy here, I

think I have all the backup I need." Betsy was a double-barreled, pearl handled 38-caliber derringer. We went to Apartment 3 and Danny pounded on the door, bellowing, "Open up this Goddamn door or we'll break it down!"

The guy inside looked through the Venetian blinds covering the window next to the door. He saw the two of us; a very angry medium sized black man and a huge white boy standing there. I'm sure we weren't a pretty sight. The door opened immediately. "You owe me $13 you low life thieving son of a bitch!"

The man produced a 5 and a 10-dollar bill. Danny snatched them away, turned on his heel and said to me "Come on, we're out of here."

As Danny was stomping down the hall with me in tow, the man still standing in his doorway cried out "Hey! What about my change?"

"Fuck you!" was Danny's reply as he shoved the bills into his pocket.

After that Danny and I were pals. Two years later, Danny was planning to take a winter vacation in Hawaii. One Saturday morning, I invited him to my house so I could lend him my commercial quality facemask, snorkel and fins. We were having some coffee when my wife Jackie came into the kitchen. Although Danny was a relatively light skinned African American he definitely had African features.

"So, Lou says you're headed to Hawaii." Jackie said after I introduced them.

"Yeah." Danny said. "I'm going to work on my tan."

Jackie is one of the brightest people I have ever known but she is not always the most observant. Danny's little joke was lost on her.

She looked at him and said. "Goodness, your plenty dark already." Danny's eyes got wider and his mouth dropped open. I made a face and tried to wave her off of this subject, but as I mentioned, Jackie is not always the most observant of people and she continued to plunge down this embarrassing verbal path.

She sat down next to Danny and put her arm next to his and said, "Look Lou.

Look how dark he is already!"

Danny cleared his throat a couple of times. "Well it sort of comes with the territory." He tried to explain. This too, was lost on Jackie. "No really." She persevered. "How do you maintain such a great tan in the middle of winter? What do you do? Go to a tanning salon?"

I could stand it no longer. I knew she wouldn't stop. "THE MAN IS BLACK!!!" I emphasized each word with a downward swing of my upturned hands.

"Oh." She said. "Oh." She said again, and finally realizing the monumental size of her social faux paux. "Danny, I am sooo SORRY."

I was horrified. Danny was laughing. He put his hand on top of hers. "It's all right Jackie. Lou has told me all about you and I know that you don't have a malicious bone in your body. But please, let me share this story with others. It's one of the funniest things that has ever happened to me."

And indeed, on more than one occasion I have had this story recounted to me by people who had previously ridden Danny.

As all of us do, Danny had some problems. About eight years later his troubles became too much for him to bear and early one terrible morning he ate his gun. It saddens me to think about losing him. He was a great guy and we had lots of good times.

Chapter 61

I had picked up my passenger at the Doubletree Inn. We were headed over to the executive airport. He had an accent and I asked if he was from the Middle East.

"I'm from Israel."

"What brings you to this neck of the woods?"

"I'm with the Israeli Consulate."

He was a diplomat. I'm afraid my next statement was less than diplomatic.

"Has it ever occurred to you guys that when you hit Palestinian refugee camps, with F-16s, tanks, and helicopters, killing innocent women and children, you're just playing into the hands of the bad guys and actually making more terrorists? What you are doing is more like reprisals, than retaliation on the actual perpetrators of these terrible outrages you have been suffering."

My unsolicited advice really pissed off my passenger. He waved the index finger of his right hand in the air.

"When it comes to Israeli security you have no right to criticize!"

"Excuse me, but I think the billions of dollars in foreign aid and military assistance we send you guys each and every year earns us the right to be critical of your actions, especially if you insist on behaving like unprincipled arrogant thugs!"

His eyes narrowed. " Oh, you don't like Jews very much do you?"

"I AM JEWISH, and you guys embarrass me.

He rode the rest of the way to the airport in fuming silence. Needless to say, I didn't receive a tip.

◆

Speaking of tips, I was driving Paul, and Doc Ben, home from the Fox & Goose, a local British style watering hole. Paul hailed from England, and Ben is a Scottish doctor. They had both been at the pub for quite some time and were having a merry ride home. It was agreed that Doc Ben would be covering the cab fare for both of them.

Ben is a charming and witty fellow, with a wonderful brogue that is music to my ears. He does however, have one character flaw from a cabdriver's perspective: He is a lousy tipper. Sometimes not tipping at all. To me this is no big deal, and I love hauling him around. Paul, on the other hand, found this facet of Doc Ben's personality to be appalling. He was concerned about the tip I would be receiving at the end of the ride.

"Now remember Ben, you're going to take care of Lou, right? For God's sakes, don't be a Jew! Make sure you tip the man! Do you hear me Ben? Don't be a Jew!

I'm not particularly sensitive about being Jewish and have rarely encountered any anti-Semitism. I did however feel compelled to say something.

"You know, that's an unfortunate

choice of words. You never can tell. Your driver might be Jewish."

I looked at Paul who was riding in the front seat. His eyes widened, his mouth dropped, and he slapped a hand to his forehead in embarrassment.

"Oh, blimey! Lou I didn't know and certainly didn't mean any offence. Believe me!"

"Hey Paul, it's a figure of speech. I didn't take it personally, I know what is in your heart and you're a good enough bloke. For crying out loud, you were just trying to get me tipped. But you might be a little more careful in the future. Some folks could take umbrage."

At this point, Doc Ben chimed in with "Are you circumcised lad?"

I wasn't particularly upset about Paul's pejorative use of the word the Jew, nor was I mad about Doc Ben asking me if I had been circumcised. But, I have been mightily pissed off for most of my 54 years on this planet, that the answer to his question is yes. Who thinks this stuff up? And even if it used to make sense, I've got a news flash for you; we're not wandering in the desert anymore. There's lots of running water. Hygiene is no longer an issue.

Let's see, we have a brand new, perfectly intact, innocent little baby boy, minding his own business, not bothering anyone. And hey, let's cut off the tip of his little pecker, without so much as a by your leave I might add. What is up with that? Not only was I mutilated shortly after birth, but as a result of that mutilation the sensitivity in that area has been greatly diminished. Thanks a lot Mom and Dad. Come on people; let's think of a better way of welcoming our little guys into this world, shall we?

Chapter 62

As soon as they got in the cab I knew I was in trouble. I had picked them up on the corner of 2nd Ave and Franklin. The vibes were really tense and I could hear her whispering to him about him doing it. I was pretty sure that "it" was robbing me. We turned left on Stockton Blvd and were headed toward G Parkway a busy-late-at-night and very dangerous neighborhood.

The FM radio was softly playing and suddenly I heard the Pointer Sisters singing Fire. Who cares that I'm about to be robbed and maybe shot? There's a great song playing. I twisted the volume nob to the right and my cab was filled with the joyous and naughty tune. I looked back at my surprised passengers and said, "I hope it's not too loud, but I just love the Pointer Sisters." I turned around and looked at him. He regarded me for a while and then replied, "No man it's OK, crank that sucker up." The next thing I know, we're all singing. We threw on some pretty good harmonies, if I do say so myself. Shortly after we finished the song, we arrived at G parkway and the moment of truth. Pull over her the large and, I assumed, heavily armed man in the back seat requested.

"Tell you what we're going to do. You are going to give us a free cab ride and we're going to let you live."

"Works for me," was my immediate reply.

As they were walking away from the cab, I called after them, "We sounded pretty good, huh?"

"Yeah, right" the man said continuing on his way, "Don't quit your day job."

I wonder what would have happened if I had been listening to Willie Nelson that almost fateful night.

Chapter 63

California prohibits the sale of alcohol after 2 A.M. Starting around 1:40 a.m. we in Cabland experience a bar rush. This can be a very busy time. If you don't have a call to run on, cruising by the drinking establishments sometimes can prove to be very lucrative. I was driving slowly through the parking lot at Charlie Brown's. It was 2:05 and there were still some folks trying for a last-minute score.

One young fellow talking to a very attractive blonde lady motioned me to stop. He came over to the cab and said through the opened driver's window, "Stick around, I might need a ride."

He walked back to the sweet young thing's car. After about 5 minutes of not quite begging he accepted the inevitable, exchanged phone numbers and disappointedly returned to my cab. He got into the front seat.

"Damn," he said. "I thought I was in."

"Well you sure gave it a good try,"

I observed. "Hell, I was rooting for you," I added less than genuinely.

He told me we were headed for Madison and Fair Oaks. I popped onto Business 80 East. I picked up my microphone and informed the dispatcher of our destination. This was always a good idea in case I ran into trouble, and it could help land me a call if one was waiting where I was dropping. My drunken passenger wanted to talk on the radio. I said he couldn't.

"I want to talk on the radio!" he insisted.

"You can't," I said once again.

"I want to talk on the radio!" he said even louder this time.

"Look Pal, what part of the sentence 'You can't' do you not understand?" I replied with no little exasperation. "If the dispatcher figures out that you're talking on my radio I can forget about making any more money on this shift."

"Yeah? Well I'll show you," was his heated reply. My demented passenger proceeded to roll down his window, crawl out of that window and, so help me God, climb onto the roof of my cab, which was traveling at 65+ m.p.h. Looking out of his open window I could see his feet dangling. Now I heard a knocking on my window. His upside-down head, hair blowing in the wind, was leering at me.

"I want to talk on the radio!" he repeated once again.

"You can't! And get off my cab, you crazy asshole" I yelled. I could see people in other cars pointing with their mouths open. This was simply not a sight folks were used to seeing. I was hoping a police, sheriff or CHP unit would drive by and shoot this maniac off my roof, but no such luck. There's never a cop around when there's a maniac on the roof of your cab.

My passenger was taking a big chance. Had I panicked and slammed on my brakes the sawdust between his ears would be spread all over Business 80. Luckily for him I kept my wits about me and gently decelerated while pulling over. My human fly companion climbed back into his seat. With a look of satisfaction on his face he said, "I'll bet no one's ever done that before."

I certainly couldn't dispute that observation. "You are without a doubt the craziest son of a bitch I've ever had in, or on my cab," I honestly replied. He liked that. My guess is he put it on his resume. Proof positive once again that the consumption of alcohol does not necessarily promote deep thinking.

Lou Solitske was born in Chicago in 1947 but he has lived most of his life in California. He graduated with a degree in Economics from San Jose State College in 1970. In 1969 he was the Northern California NCAA heavy weight brown belt Judo champion. In 1975 he found a woman who would actually be seen in public with him and was gratefully married ever after. He was a Yellow Cab driver in Sacramento from 1987 to 2005 and was the primary ground transportation resource for all UPS Air Operations in the Sacramento area. He has been invited to read his poetry at regional events and has been interviewed numerous times by local publications and television stations as he is considered by many to be the best cab driver in Sacramento and was so named in 2001 by Sacramento News and Review. In 2005, Lou retired and moved to Half Moon Bay, California with his wife Jackie and two poodles. He currently lives in Seaside Oregon with his grumpy old cat.

Made in the USA
San Bernardino, CA
22 December 2016